Praise for

# THINGS THAT

T0044384

"Packed with insights and practical e: points the way to free ourselves from ev. possessions, past mistakes, applause, and fear—so that we can build the lives we seek to create."

—GRETCHEN RUBIN, author of
*The Happiness Project* and *Better Than Before*

"Joshua Becker is inviting you to live a more real and rewarding life—not through consuming, competing, or completely overhauling your life—but rather by making simple yet impactful, daily actions. The thought-provoking insights and touching, relatable, personal stories inside *Things That Matter* will help you live your one precious life with more presence, purpose, and peace."

—RACHEL MACY STAFFORD, *New York Times* bestselling author of
*Hands Free Mama* and *Only Love Today*

"*Things That Matter* is a must-read to re-center yourself and filter out the distractions of the world. When you discover what matters most to you, everything else falls into its proper place."

—CHRIS NORTON, motivational keynote speaker
featured in the documentary *7 Yards*

"This book is a balm for the soul. Reminding us that chasing fame and fortune squanders our precious life energy, Joshua offers a compassionate guide to finding what really matters."

—ROBERT J. WALDINGER, MD, professor of psychiatry
at Harvard Medical School

"This book gives you both personal and practical advice on how to face past mistakes—no matter what area of your life they may encompass. Joshua shares his insight from the perspective of a friend who truly cares and who wants to help you move beyond the regret-and-avoidance cycle into purposeful living."

—DAWN MADSEN, The Minimal Mom and author of
*Declutter Your Home in 15 Minutes a Day*

"A must-read for anyone looking to regain control of life. This delightful guide full of impactful and practical information will lead you through many of the roadblocks you may be facing."

—RONALD L. BANKS, speaker, writer, and coach

"*Things That Matter* is required reading for anyone seeking practical guidance on how to confront life's many distractions and—more importantly—how to overcome them."

—CHRISTINE PLATT, author of
*The Afrominimalist's Guide to Living with Less*

"By removing the distractions outlined in this book, we are able to clear the clutter and create space to build life balance, personal growth, and purpose."

—DAVE BRAUN AND TROY AMDAHL (THE OOLAGUYS),
cofounders of oolalife.com, international
bestselling authors, and experts on work-life balance

"This book's siren call—that we should aim to be generous, not wealthy, and get dirt under our fingernails by serving others—cements Joshua's status as a much-needed voice of reason and kindness in the modern world."

—HELEN RUSSELL, bestselling author of *How to Be Sad*

"Every once in a while you read a book that can save you years (or decades) of angst, disappointment, and missed attempts at finding significance and contentment. This is one of those books, packed with wisdom and insight."

—CAREY NIEUWHOF, bestselling author, speaker, and podcast host

"Joshua's work and this book are a beautiful combination of wisdom, warmth, and practical advice to help us live with intention and meaning. We have the power to make choices every day to do more of what truly matters—and Joshua offers us practical suggestions to do this."

—NATALY KOGAN, bestselling author of *The Awesome Human Project* and *Happier Now*

"Ten years from now it won't really matter what shoes you wore today, how your hair looked, or what brand of clothes you wore. What will matter is how you lived, how you loved, and what you learned along the way. And *Things That Matter* is a beautiful guide for getting there."

—MARC AND ANGEL CHERNOFF, *New York Times* bestselling authors of *Getting Back to Happy* and *1000+ Little Things Happy Successful People Do Differently*

# THINGS
# THAT MATTER

# THINGS
# THAT MATTER

*Overcoming Distraction
to Pursue a More Meaningful Life*

## JOSHUA BECKER
with Eric Stanford

WATERBROOK

Published in the United States by WaterBrook, an imprint of Random House, a division of Penguin Random House LLC.

WATERBROOK and colophon are registered trademarks of Penguin Random House LLC.

Originally published in hardcover and in slightly different form by WaterBrook, an imprint of Random House, a division of Penguin Random House LLC, in 2022.

Trade Paperback ISBN 978-0-593-19399-0
Ebook ISBN 978-0-593-19398-3

The Cataloging-in-Publication Data is on file with the Library of Congress at https://lccn.loc.gov/2021030961.

Printed in the United States of America on acid-free paper

waterbrookmultnomah.com

2 4 6 8 9 7 5 3 1

Most WaterBrook books are available at special quantity discounts for bulk purchase for premiums, fundraising, and corporate and educational needs by organizations, churches, and businesses. Special books or book excerpts also can be created to fit specific needs. For details, contact specialmarketscms@penguinrandomhouse.com.

For my grandfather Rev. Harold E. Salem

# CONTENTS

**PART 4      ENDING OF THE BOOK, BEGINNING
             OF A MORE MEANINGFUL LIFE**

# PART 1

## THE OBJECTIVE AND THE OBSTACLES

# 1

## A Life with No Regrets

### *Beginning with a View to the End*

We are not given a short life but we make it short, and
we are not ill-supplied but wasteful of it. . . .
Life is long if you know how to use it.

         —SENECA, "ON THE SHORTNESS OF LIFE"

Bronnie Ware, an Australian nurse who spent several years caring for people during the last weeks of their lives, routinely asked her patients about any regrets they had or anything they would do differently if they could. Later she posted an article called "Regrets of the Dying" about her findings. In it, Ware wrote of the phenomenal clarity of vision that people gained at the end of their lives as well as the common themes that surfaced again and again during these conversations. This article has been shared millions of times online and was turned into a book in 2012.[1]

It's a fascinating premise, isn't it? What do people most regret about their lives?

I'm not going to include the list here. Instead, I want to ask you: How badly do you want to know what's on it? How tempted are you to google the article right now so you can see the top regrets that people have at the end of their lives? And more importantly, where does that desire to know the regrets of the dying come from? Isn't the strength of your interest proof that you're concerned that *your* life might be wasted?

(Now that I've got you thinking about that, if you still want to know what the list is, you can turn to the first endnote at the back of this book and find the list there.)

Why did a list about other people's dying regrets go viral? It's because we all know that's going to be us nearing death someday and we don't want to have regrets when we get there. And also, I believe, because *we're already starting to have regrets about our life choices.*

For people in middle age, and even for people in young adulthood, it's common to have nagging anxiety that we're squandering our time and resources on things that are not important while not focusing enough on the things and people that really do matter. And we can easily imagine that we'll be sorry about it someday if we don't make a change. Yet on and on we go, putting the inconsequential ahead of the imperative.

---

## On and on we go, putting the inconsequential ahead of the imperative.

---

Something's got to change here. And there's only so much time ahead in each of our lives to make the change.

We're always going to make some foolish decisions along the way that we wish we could take back. So it's probably not possible to live a life with absolutely *no* regrets. But it most certainly *is* possible to make changes that take us off the easy path of immersing ourselves in the ordinary and the immediate and put us onto a more intentional path that leads to a life that satisfies and resonates beyond our own mortal existence—a life well lived. Presented with the choice, don't we all want a life of fewer regrets and more fulfillment?

One day, not long ago, I was forced to come face to face with something I just *had to do* before I died. And I want to tell you about it now, because it's related to you.

## One Thing

In October 2019, I sat with a number of team members from my staff at a conference called Start Finishing, at the K'é Main Street Learning Lab in Mesa, Arizona. Charlie Gilkey, author of a book with the same title as the conference, was our presenter for the day. Charlie told us he wanted us to be specific in applying the principles of the workshop to the most important work in our lives. To help us determine what that work was, he said, "Close your eyes and answer this question: If you were to die today, what is the one project you would be most disappointed that you weren't able to complete?"

After asking ourselves the question, we shared around the table what work we saw as most important. The young woman next to me mentioned an art project she wanted to complete. A mother of two spoke about her desire to prepare her two teenagers for life. For me, without hesitation, I answered Charlie's question this way: "If I were to die today, I would be most disappointed that I never got a chance to write that book I've been thinking about for a long time now."

I bet you can guess what book it was.

It's the one you're reading right now.

For a while, I'd been thinking about writing a book that takes the principles of minimalism I am known for and paints a bigger picture of how distractions keep us from meaning, purpose, and satisfaction. And at that very moment in the Learning Lab, writing *Things That*

*Matter* became my highest-priority task. Because there is one message that drives me more than any other—and it's not helping people clean out their closets, as useful as that is. The one message that burns most in my heart is the invitation to live an intentional, meaningful life. Apart from my faith and my family, this message is what I most want to be remembered for after I'm gone.

I've been reading and writing and talking about this subject for years, which has given me the opportunity to pick up many viewpoints and stories. Now I'm bringing all the most important insights together in one volume, focusing especially on how to achieve the focus that is required to live according to your priorities. In *Things That Matter*, I want to show you what you need to clear away from your life to transition to more intentional living.

Living a life of purpose is important not just to me or to a few others like me. It's important to all of us, because we all have at least one thing (probably more) that we feel we just *have to do* before we die. And I'm not talking about bucket-list items like "ride in a hot-air balloon." I'm talking about living in a way that makes a difference. I'm talking about knowing our lives matter and make an impact on the world in a positive way, that our existences mean something.

This brings me to you. Let me ask you the same question Charlie Gilkey asked me: If you were to die today, what one thing (or few things) would you be most disappointed that you weren't able to complete? Please don't just cruise past that question. Stop and think about it. Identify your top-level goals, clearly and specifically.

---

If you were to die today, what
one thing (or few things) would
you be most disappointed that
you weren't able to complete?

---

In preparation for writing this book, I commissioned a nationally representative poll—the Things That Matter Survey—that asked a number of questions related to the themes of this book.[2] I'll be referring to the survey findings regularly in the chapters to come, and I believe you'll find the results fascinating. To start with, one question we asked was "Would you say that you have identified a clear purpose, or purposes, for your life?" I was pleased to see that 70 percent of respondents answered yes. Another 19 percent answered no, while 11 percent were unsure.

Would you say that you have identified a clear purpose, or purposes, for your life?

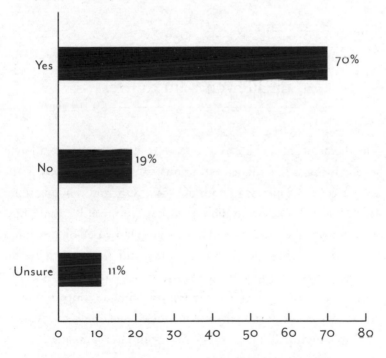

Do you know your purpose or purposes? If the answer is no or you are unsure (like 30 percent of the poll participants), I invite you to go to the "Discover Your Purposes" exercise at the end of this book. It will help you methodically think through the desires that land at the intersection of your passions, your abilities, and the needs of the world. You'll see what works of service you're suited for and drawn toward doing.

If you're a part of the 70 percent and you think you know your purpose, that's wonderful. Nevertheless, I encourage you to keep your mind open, because this book most likely will help you refine or redefine the things that matter to you along the way.

Right now, I want you to start believing that it's *not too late* to reorient your life around your purposes. You can do something *now* to live the life you want to live and eventually come to the end with fewer regrets.

---

## You can do something *now* to live the life you want to live.

---

The theme of this book isn't a "how to be happy" message, though I believe living a life aligned with your values and passions is the quickest way to happiness in both the short term and the long term. This book is about so much more than how you feel; it's about how you live the one life you have and how to keep it focused on the things that matter. I would go so far as to say the world *needs* you to live for the things that matter to you because you're at your most productive and influential self when you're offering your unique contribution.

There may be no greater pursuit for yourself *and* others than choosing to live a meaningful life focused on the things that matter.

## How to Make Your Life Long Enough

In college, I had a professor who taught, "Make a point to read books from previous centuries, because all living writers are swimming in the same cultural and ideological currents. But a book from centuries ago will come from a different perspective and will challenge your thinking in new ways."

I've tried to live by that advice. In fact, a lot of my ideas about God, minimalism, living with purpose, and other subjects close to my heart have been informed by wise men and women of past ages. They bring a fresh perspective in a way that modern scholars or pundits can't. And I've found that themes echoed repeatedly in different eras and in different places are often themes that can still show us the way to a better life.

With that in mind, I want to share with you a quote that has meant a great deal to me for many years now. It's from Seneca the Younger, a Roman philosopher born about the same time as Jesus of Nazareth.

> It is not that we have a short time to live, but that we waste a lot of it. Life is long enough, and a sufficiently generous amount has been given to us for the highest achievements if it were all well invested. But when it is wasted in heedless luxury and spent on no good activity, we are forced at last by death's final constraint to realize that it has passed away before we knew it was passing. So it is: we are not given a short life but we make it short, and we are not ill-supplied but wasteful of it. . . .
> Life is long if you know how to use it.[3]

There's a lot in that excerpt. I'd urge you to reread it, and maybe even get out a pen and underline key phrases that stick out to you. Start with "we waste a lot of it."

Seneca's bold claim is what I'm talking about when I refer to intentional living. It's living on purpose. It's spending our limited time on "the highest achievements" instead of on "heedless luxury" and "no good activity." Because if we do that, then we'll find life is long enough to do what matters most.

---

## How we get to the end of our lives with minimal regrets: *We choose well. We set aside lesser pursuits to seek meaning in our lives. And we do it every single day.*

---

Seneca points us to the answer to the conundrum of how we get to the end of our lives with minimal regrets: *We choose well. We set aside lesser pursuits to seek meaning in our lives. And we do it every single day.*

## Becoming Meaningful

---

For me, learning how to live my life on purpose was not an instantaneous epiphany, although there were plenty of light-bulb moments along the way. It was more of a gradual growth in understanding, influenced by the things going on in my life over many years.

My faith upbringing primed me for thinking about priorities and pursuing the important things in life. It caused me to focus on issues of what matters for eternity and what does not. Then, as a young man, I became a pastor and spent my time helping others find their way in life through biblical teaching. So I've got to give my family and my faith tradition a lot of credit for attuning me to the issues we're talking about in this book. (By the way, *Things That Matter* is not a religious book, but because my faith has shaped me, I will mention my own religious history from time to time.) Despite the benefits in my background, it wasn't until after I'd become a minimalist in my early thirties that my mental space was freed up, and even forced, to really face questions of priority.

If you've read any of my books or blog posts over the last dozen-plus years, you know how important simple living is to me.[4] In fact, one of my greatest passions in life is to inspire and help people to own less stuff. Minimalism is one thing that matters greatly to me. Nevertheless, to me, minimalism has always been a means, not an end in itself.

I define *minimalism* as "the intentional promotion of the things we most value by removing anything that distracts us from them." It isn't negative; it's positive. It isn't primarily about decluttering or organizing; it's about creating freedom. Because when we own fewer possessions, we liberate precious energy, time, and focus that we can direct toward more meaningful pursuits.

I've experienced the benefits of this reality in my own life. Minimalism gave me the ability to really explore the topic of significant living in myself and in what I was seeing in the world. I began thinking, *Accumulating more and more possessions is a foolish pursuit, when you think about it, but it's not the only foolish pursuit in life. So what are some of the other distractions that I see in my life? Or in the lives of people close to me? Is it possible to live life with fewer regrets? And if so, what keeps people from a fulfilled life in ways they aren't even noticing?*

Gradually, I began experimenting with my newfound freedom to see what I could do that helped other people and brought me joy. And in all honesty, since my family discarded the majority of our possessions in 2008, I've accomplished way more with my life than I ever thought I would. It's not because I'm special. It's because I'm intentional.

May I share a few highlights?

It all started with a blog, *Becoming Minimalist*, that chronicled my journey and thoughts since the first week I started minimizing. That blog has now reached sixty million people with the life-changing message of owning less. I started a Facebook page, also called *Becoming Minimalist*, that now reaches over fifty million people every month. My YouTube channel accounts for millions of minutes watched every month. I've written four books, started two digital magazines, developed a mobile app, and created an online course called Uncluttered that has helped over seventy thousand families declutter their homes. I've traveled the world speaking, have been featured in several documentaries, and have been interviewed or published in major media outlets around the world.

It's been quite a ride. But I don't share those facts with a prideful attitude (although I *am* proud of them). I share those accomplishments to make a point: I believe, beyond the semblance of a doubt, that my accomplishments over the last few years are *directly* related to my pursuit of a life focused on the things that I believe truly matter.

---

> My accomplishments over the last few years are *directly* related to my pursuit of a life focused on the things that I believe truly matter.

---

For example, as an outcome of my success in promoting minimalism, in 2015, I founded and funded a nonprofit organization called the Hope Effect that is working to change how the world cares for orphans. We work with local and state governments in developing nations to find solutions for orphan care that focus on placing children in loving families rather than institutional care. At the time of this writing, we are working in six cities around the world to better care for orphaned children.

While each of us is gifted with different passions, a different personality, and different capabilities, having a life lived with focus on the things that matter most will *always* result in more accomplishments and fulfillment than we ever thought possible. This has been true for me and it can be true for you, even though the specific accomplishments will vary greatly. And the net result of it all is a life with more quiet satisfaction and less anxious regret.

It *is* possible to live this kind of life. I've experienced it myself—and I've witnessed it in the life of my own personal hero.

## A Well-Lived Life

In 2012, my ninety-year-old grandfather, Harold Salem, called me into his office. I knew this office well. Grandpa had pastored the same church in South Dakota for fifty-three years, and the items in his office always stayed the same: the large wooden desk, the typewriter, the bookshelves, even the drawer where he hid his candy. I would stop in to visit every time I was in town.

But being specifically requested to meet Grandpa in his office on a designated day at a designated time was new. I sensed that this conversation would not be filled with laughter and jokes or conversations about his beloved Minnesota Twins baseball team. But I didn't know why he had invited me. And he wouldn't tell me until I sat down across from him at his desk.

He started our conversation like this: "Joshua, I would like you to read Scripture at my funeral. Here is the verse I would like, and this is where it will take place in the service." He slid a sheet of paper toward me, labeled "Memorial Service for Harold Salem." The specific passage from the Bible I would read was clearly marked, as were the names of everyone else involved in the service. Even the number of minutes set aside for each element was clearly listed. It was a sobering moment to be previewing the funeral service for a healthy man sitting right in front of me.

The fact that my grandfather had planned his own funeral was not surprising to me. He was that type of guy. As a pastor for more than seventy years, he had participated in countless memorial services, and I'm sure he saw along the way how making specific requests about your service is helpful to those who eventually plan it.

What surprised me most about that moment, to the point that it has stuck with me years later, was the confidence with which my grandfather approached not just his funeral but also the end of his life. With assurance in his eyes, he talked about the life he had lived, the work he had accomplished, and his desire to be reunited with his wife of more than fifty years. My grandfather did not regret, in any visible way, the coming end to his days on earth. And let me tell you, there are few things in life more inspirational than peering into the eyes of a man who does not fear his own death.

Grandpa lived to be ninety-nine, mentally sharp and still working till the very end. In December 2020, he passed away after a brief battle with pneumonia. While accommodating coronavirus restrictions in place at the time, we held his funeral as he'd planned it. And that day, in my eulogy, I told the listeners about Grandpa's example of living in such a way that you need have few regrets.

His life was long enough, as Seneca declared, because he knew how to use it.

---

## The One Sentence You Need Each Day to Set Your Intention

A former mentor of mine, Robert Thune Sr., was the first person to share the idea with me. He said, "Every morning, before I start my day, I set my intention with a simple sentence that goes like this: 'Today, I commit myself to _____.'" I follow this advice, and I think you should try it too.

The blank gets to be filled in however you choose. For example:

- Today, I commit myself to *being the best mother I can be.*
- Today, I commit myself to *being a faithful spouse.*
- Today, I commit myself to *healthy eating.*
- Today, I commit myself to *selflessness.*
- Today, I commit myself to *praying whenever I feel anxious.*
- Today, I commit myself to *my work goal.*
- Today, I commit myself to *getting out of debt.*

We approach our important life objectives one day at a time. Start with a commitment just for today and see how it goes. If necessary, you can change it as soon as tomorrow.

---

## Don't Be Left Behind

Often we hear about the regrets of the dying, and we are warned to avoid making their mistakes. But rarely are we offered the alternative. Rarely are we provided with an example of a man or woman who faces death with few regrets. When we do, we are wise to follow their example and make the adjustments that will prepare us to face our own mortality with courage and confidence. My grandfather is such a person for me.

One of the most important things Grandpa did for me was teach me to spend my time on things that meet the needs of others. Certainly there's nothing wrong with spending time enjoying a sunset, getting together for coffee with a friend, or painting a watercolor, just because you want to. In fact, I promote minimalism in part so that people have the margin to relax and appreciate the little moments of joy or beauty in life. But our self-focused pursuits don't need to, and shouldn't, exclude others-focused pursuits. In the end, pursuits that help other people are the most influential, the most enduring, and even—I would say—the most rewarding for us.

---

## Pursuits that help other people are the most influential, the most enduring, and even—I would say—the most rewarding for us.

---

I hope you have a model of meaningful service to others in your life. But even if you don't, you can become a model for others by setting an example of putting aside less important pursuits to go after those things that really matter. This is the way to avoid regret. Now is the time to start.

You were designed to achieve great things! You are unique in your being, your personality, your abilities, and your relationships. And there is no one else on the face of the earth who can live your life and accomplish your good. Please do not forget that.

There is no doubt that *success* and *achievement* are relative words, and your highest achievement is different from someone else's. You may never lead thousands or cure cancer or start a nonprofit. But make no mistake: there is a good that you are designed to bring into this world that only you can accomplish, and there are people in your life whom you can serve and love better than anyone else can. Read that sentence again. *There are people in your life whom you can serve and love better than anyone else can.*

Your highest achievement will be different from mine, but we both have one. And life is long enough for us to achieve it. Regret is not inevitable.

## The Enemy

Now we have to ask a tough question: If pursuing things that matter is so great, why aren't more of us actually going after our dearest goals? Why aren't we focusing on our purposes, which would give us joy and fulfillment day by day, leading to a sense of satisfaction at the end of life?

In a word, because of *distractions.*

Things get in the way.

They might be things that apparently have to be done right away. Or things that we just assume we should do because everybody else is doing them. Or things that we'd like to escape if only we knew how. Or things that are mildly rewarding while being easy and safe. But they aren't things that matter.

The enemy of intentionality and a life well lived is distraction. Know your enemy.

# 2

---

## Distracted from Meaning

### *Letting the Lesser Crowd Out the Greater*

What distracts us will begin to define us.

—Bob Goff

Today, to an extent never before known, we are distracted by the trivial, the novel, and the (seemingly) urgent. Every day we wake to limitless information and 24/7 communication. The dentist's office wants you to reply "YES" to confirm your appointment. Flash sale—take advantage now! An email preview pops up in the corner of your screen. News of a tragedy that just took place on the other side of the world. Celebrity gossip. Beeps, ringtones, notifications, calendar reminders, and vibrations. What a person on the other political side said in reply to the person on your political side. The latest post from *Becoming Minimalist* (no, wait, that's a *good* distraction).

Where was I?

Oh yes, we're distracted by the trivial, the novel, and the urgent.

We'll be getting to the topic of distraction by social media, information, and entertainment in chapter 10. Before we get to that, however, there is a more important conversation we need to have. Because the truth is, the distractions coming from our phones, computers, and other electronic devices are far from being the whole problem when it comes to our getting derailed from the things that matter most to us and the world around us.

Our newer tech- and media-based distractions are actually just add-ons to many of the old diversions that have plagued humanity for countless generations, like having mixed-up priorities or viewing ourselves and other people in unhelpful ways. They're internal before they're external. These kinds of distractions are ones we tend to overlook, yet I would argue that they actually present the more serious obstacles to living for things that matter. So, from now on, here is where I'm going to be focusing much of my attention (and yours). We've got to look to what's going on in our hearts if we're going to open up a pathway to pursue our souls' greatest desires. This isn't a book about blaming external circumstances; this is a book about looking inward.

Let me prove to you that distraction is not just a modern-day experience—and that resisting it is a battle worth fighting.

## A Very Brief History of Distraction

Seneca—the same Roman philosopher who told us in chapter 1 that life can be long enough—also said, "There is never a time when new distractions will not come up; we sow them, and so several will grow from one seed."[1]

Distraction from a meaningful life is a crop that has been growing abundantly as long as there have been human beings. And for just as long, people have been trying to figure out how to get their distractions under control.

- In ancient Greece's golden age, the philosopher Socrates criticized writing things down by hand, because he believed it distracted people from pure thinking.

- Around 366 BCE, a young Athenian named Demosthenes, wanting to develop the skills of oratory, shut out distractions by building an underground study where he could practice speaking. (He also shaved half his head so that he would be too embarrassed to go out in public.)[2]
- Anthony the Great, a famous "desert monk" of the early Christian era, lived alone in an abandoned Roman fort in Egypt for twenty years to avoid temptation and devote himself to prayer.
- In a medical textbook published in 1775, German physician Melchior Adam Weikard diagnosed "lack of attention" as a medical condition and prescribed remedies such as sour milk, steel powder, and horseback riding.[3]
- Some of today's Silicon Valley engineers and business leaders take regular small doses of LSD or magic mushrooms, believing it focuses the mind and makes them more productive.[4]

Reading that human beings have struggled with distraction since well before the first social media post or the birth of the smartphone reminds us that the focused pursuit of things that matter is a calling in each of our lives. We can also find encouragement in knowing that others have overcome distraction to live meaningful lives, because that means we can too.

## When a Distraction Becomes a Lifestyle

In the Things That Matter Survey, we asked, "Do you feel that you are spending your time and resources on less important pursuits at the expense of things that matter most to you?" More than three-quarters—76 percent—of respondents answered, "Yes, distractions keep me from important pursuits." (Specifically, 40 percent answered

"Sometimes," 20 percent answered "Frequently," and—saddest of all—
16 percent answered "Always.")

Do you feel that you are spending your time and resources on less
important pursuits at the expense of things that matter most to you?

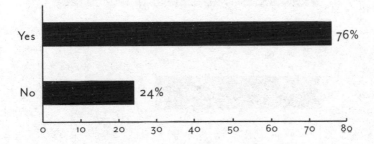

We also asked, "Are these distractions becoming a bigger or smaller
problem in your life?" Over half—52 percent—said that distractions
from their highest priorities were growing, while 32 percent said the
distractions were decreasing. (The remaining respondents were unsure.)

My takeaway from this? Distraction is a big problem that isn't getting any better, and we are well aware of it.

Now, of course, not all distractions are wrong all the time. Many
times, there's nothing wrong with doing things that divert our
minds—watching a TV show, or reading a novel, or gardening, or
whatever else entertains or relaxes us. Sometimes we need distraction from our labors or our problems—that's when distractions are
good.

But distractions have a dual character. "The only thing that con-
soles us for our miseries is diversion," said seventeenth century poly-
math Blaise Pascal. "And yet it is the greatest of our miseries. For it is
that above all which prevents us thinking about ourselves and leads us
imperceptibly to destruction."[5]

Are these distractions becoming a bigger or smaller problem in your life?

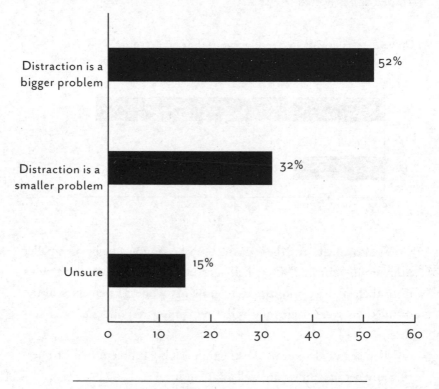

When a distraction becomes a
lifestyle, we lose control over the
life we are living.

The problem begins when distractions take over our lives and push out more important pursuits. Indulging in distractions can go from being an occasional pastime to becoming an ingrained part of our lifestyles. This is what happens when we spend all our spare time gaming. Or we exercise so much that our working out doesn't give us energy; it uses up our energy. Or we shop for hours because we don't want to go home. Or career ambitions become workaholism. If this kind of behavior continues, then we're at risk of getting to the end of our lives and wondering, *Why did I waste this life on things that don't matter? I wish I had more time.*

When a distraction becomes a lifestyle, we lose control over the lives we are living. We lose intentionality.

## How Distractions Take Over a Life

Few distractions *begin* as a lifestyle. At first, they are simply fun and interesting. We enjoy the new game, the new television show, the new hobby, or the new website. We like the new phone, the new store, or the new idea that could become the new money-making opportunity in our lives.

Some things we are drawn to quicker than others. But for the most part, the shiny new object is just a welcome distraction from the hard task of living life.

Slowly, however, the new distraction begins to take more time and more energy from us. We get better at it, or invest more into it, or find increased enjoyment in it, or start to make money from it. We begin to make accommodations to partake in it even more.

Soon we rationalize why it's good to do even more of it. We steal a few extra minutes here or there to enjoy it. But the number of hours in the day never changes. So eventually we start to sacrifice the most important things in order to indulge ourselves even more in the distraction. Before we know it, this has become a way of life, not a welcome diversion from our problems.

The *distraction* has now become a *lifestyle* . . . and we have lost some of our control over the lives we are living because of it.

Sometimes we recognize this right away and course-correct. But other times, years are wasted, relationships are lost, and purpose is slowly, subtly frittered away.

With risks like these, distraction should be a greater concern to us than it usually is.

## How to Put Distractions in Their Place

How can we respond when distractions have become our masters rather than our servants?

First, we can be vigilant in self-examination. We ought to frequently sit quietly with ourselves, examining the trajectory of our lives and the distractions that keep us from being the best version of ourselves. The next eight chapters will be an aid in self-examination for you.

Second, we can verbally articulate what distractions are keeping us from our best work, keeping us from those we love the most, or keeping us from fulfilling our highest purpose. As I mentioned, these distractions may not always be unhealthy on the surface—but if they have spilled into places where they do not belong, they may become so.

Third, we can be diligent and intentional in removing these distractions. This can be difficult and requires moments of wrestling within ourselves. But learn to fight.

Last, it is important to remind ourselves of the value of the most important duties in front of us. Your most important work will never be the easiest—in fact, it will probably be one of the hardest things you ever do. Being an intentional parent, loving spouse, faithful employee, inspirational artist, good boss, or selfless member of a community is never the easiest road to travel. But in the long run, there is more joy and happiness to be found there than anywhere else.

Distractions don't get to define you. *You* get to define you.

And some of the most admirable men and women I know were people brave enough to course-correct from one lifestyle to more important goals.

## Five O'Clock Shift Change

Retired now, Ed Townley used to be an executive with Agri-Mark, a dairy co-op in the northeastern United States best known for its Cabot cheese products. Back when I lived in Vermont, I knew him as a loving father to two adopted boys, a faithful husband, and a member of several nonprofit boards, including that of the Special Olympics.

Ed had risen to his position of CFO at Agri-Mark by devoting long hours, along with his considerable talents, to his job. One thing that mattered greatly to both him and his wife in their young-adult years was business success, and Ed pursued it aggressively. He was good at his job, was dedicated to his tasks, and saw his work as service to farmers and customers.

But he realized that the focus of his energy would need to be realigned when he and his wife, Jennifer, adopted their second child.

"I'd been living my life one way, for many years," he told me in a recent phone conversation, "but I quickly saw that my wife needed a new Ed. And I knew the responsibility that would be required at home."

So Ed pursued the kind of life realignment that few are brave enough to muster.

"I went to my boss one day and said simply this: 'You know that since I started working here I've been the first to arrive, sometimes the last to leave, and almost always available to work on weekends when needed. But my responsibilities at home have changed with our second child. From here on, I'm going to leave at five o'clock every evening without fail. Jennifer needs me at home. Of course, I'll still give you everything I've got while I'm here. But my values have realigned.'"

Ed had trepidation in his heart when he made this statement. Would his boss be offended? Would he get fired or lose any chance of further advancement?

Nothing like that happened. The boss understood and agreed to the change.

In fact, not only did his boss understand, so did the other people in the office. "My coworkers knew that every day I was leaving at five. And they learned to respect it—quickly, as a matter of fact. If they needed something from me, they couldn't walk in my office at five minutes to five. They learned to ask earlier."

Regardless of the career sacrifice he might be making, Ed knew it was the right decision. His career could no longer be the sole determinant of his lifestyle. There were more important responsibilities now.

Years after that turning point in Ed's life, I asked him, "Did you stick to that decision?"

"Joshua," he said, "I never once stayed in the office past five from that day on. In fact, when I became CEO, the company moved their annual business meeting to accommodate my decision."

His work was still important to him. But *over*working would draw him away from a higher priority—his family. And he was brave enough to course-correct.

Ed continued to flourish in his job, finishing his career as the head of Agri-Mark. More importantly, his family also flourished. Something new that mattered greatly to him had come along, and he had changed his priorities to focus on it.

## The Challenge Is Great, but the Rewards Are Greater

Distractions are here, and they're never going away. That means it's never too early and never too late to learn how to say no to them over and over again.

Each of the following eight chapters addresses one distraction that keeps us from living a life with more meaning and fewer regrets.

1. *The distraction of fear.* So many people never start chasing their dreams, or quit too soon, because they're scared of something.

2. *The distraction of past mistakes.* For many people, never getting past ways they have messed up or wrongs others have done to them prevents them from making progress on things that matter to them.

3. *The distraction of happiness.* When we try to satisfy our pursuit of happiness in the pursuit of self, we always fall short of the truest, most lasting forms of happiness.

4. *The distraction of money.* The desire for money causes many to sacrifice their true passions and objectives just to acquire more of it.

5. *The distraction of possessions.* All that stuff we own is constantly calling out for our attention.

6. *The distraction of applause.* Finding our self-worth in the approval of others negatively impacts the decisions we make and the lives we choose to live.

7. *The distraction of leisure.* Many of us are more focused on getting to our weekends, vacations, and retirement than on doing things we're passionate about.

8. *The distraction of technology.* Here's a problem that characterizes practically all of us in this tech-saturated age—all those posts, notifications, reminders, headlines, and ringtones.

Of course, these eight are not the only distractions we face, but these are some that I see coming up over and over again. They are also distractions that are powerful enough to derail us from achieving our most cherished goals and purposes.

I will be presenting pivotal principles for overcoming each of these distractions. As you can see from the list above, these are not easy distractions to overcome. This book is about more than tying a rubber band around your phone so you use it less. The steps I present are guidance for doing the hard work of eliminating personal, societal, and cultural distractions. We wage war every single day to defeat these distractions and align ourselves with greater pursuits.

But remember, the pursuit of things that matter is about making the most of your life and discovering fulfillment. So while clearing away the distractions may seem like a sacrifice, it's actually an endeavor that pays off in the long run. You can begin to feel more satisfied and less regretful about your life this very day if you just make a decision to live for things and people that matter.

I believe very few people want to waste the one life they've been given. Most *want* to focus on things that matter. So the problem is not that we don't have a passion for meaning; the problem is that our focus is so often distracted from it.

---

The problem is not that we don't have a passion for meaning; the problem is that our focus is so often distracted from it.

---

It has been said, "The two most important days in your life are the day you are born and the day you discover the reason why."[6] I like to add a third: the day you throw off the distractions that keep you from it.

Are you ready to deal with your distractions?

## Jump While You Can

A few years ago, I spent a week with my family in Costa Rica. There is much to see and do in that beautiful country, and my wife and I and both of our kids (eleven and fifteen at the time) thoroughly enjoyed the trip.

One afternoon, we went on a catamaran ride to look for dolphins, witness the sunset, and enjoy dinner out on the ocean. At one scenic stop on the tour, the boat anchored and the captain invited everyone to disembark for snorkeling and swimming.

In addition, the captain invited people to jump off the top deck of the catamaran into the ocean if they wanted. As you might imagine, the teenage boys and young adults were the first to attempt the high dive into the water below. Some needed a little peer pressure, but most of the young men were more than happy to jump (and try to impress the girls they brought with them).

While the boat was anchored, I looked around at the other participants on the tour and for the first time noticed how many elderly people were on board. They were enjoying the scenery but clearly had no intention of getting off to swim or snorkel, much less jump twenty-five feet off the top of the boat into the water below.

Interrupting my thoughts, my wife asked if I was going to jump with the others.

"Yes," I said. "I'm going to jump . . . while I still can."

I was forty-three at the time, healthy, and in fairly good shape. There will probably come a day when I am unable to jump twenty-five feet from a boat. But that was not the day. On that day, I could jump. So I decided I would.

There are moments in life whose significance is difficult to communicate adequately with words. The circumstances are just right; the emotions are in perfect alignment; the will is there. This was one of those times for me. I just had to jump. I didn't want to regret missing my opportunity.

Maybe this is that kind of time for you when it comes to changing your focus and living more intentionally for things that matter. Maybe it's time for you to jump while you can.

# PART 2

---

# DISTRACTIONS OF A
# PARALYZED WILL

# 3

## Dreams Overshadowed

### Overcoming the Distraction of Fear

Twenty years from now you will be more disappointed by
the things you didn't do than by the ones you did.
—SARAH FRANCES BROWN

A sharp and attractive young woman in her early twenties, Taylor
works in the perfume department of a large store in Santa Monica to
pay off her student loans and other bills. She appreciates the job and
is doing her best at it, but it isn't the kind of work she wants to do long
term.

Early in her stint at the perfume counter, Taylor took advantage of a
lull in customer traffic to get to know another salesperson better. They
shared a little of their stories with each other. Taylor said to the other
woman, "What I really want to do is graphic design. That's what I studied for in college, and that's what I love. I've already got some part-time
gigs designing websites. It's only a matter of time until I've got enough
prospects to take the leap and quit this job so I can focus on running my
own studio and help people with their graphic-design needs."

The other salesperson, Jiao, seemed interested yet solemn while listening to Taylor's plans. "I admire you for chasing your dreams," Jiao
said. "I wish I had. You know, I never thought I would be thirty-nine
and still doing this."

"Well, why don't you try something else?" asked Taylor.

"No, no, it's too late." Jiao walked off.

Taylor is a friend of mine, and she told me about this conversation. "I felt sorry for her," Taylor explained. "It's like she would rather be miserable than uncomfortable."

I don't know anything about Jiao's history, and it's not my place to judge her, but I recognize the scenario Taylor described. So many people would rather be disappointed and unfulfilled doing things that are safe than go through the anxiety of chasing valuable dreams and goals. Sadly, they prefer a safe, meaningless status quo over taking a risk that might lead to failure—*or* might lead to success.

Perhaps if they factored in the potential of massive regret before the end of life, it would be enough to help them choose risk over the rut they're stuck in. And let's face it, some pursuits in life are worth risk.

## Fears That Keep Us from Trying

On one hand, there is such a thing as good fear. A healthy dose of caution can keep you from doing things you would later regret. But on the other hand, there is also bad fear. A sign of maturity is learning to distinguish between the two.

So many people never even take the first step toward what they consider meaningful in life because they think it will be too difficult to accomplish. Or they make only half-hearted attempts that are doomed to failure, which amounts to not trying. Something is preventing them from going for it, and it's usually some form of bad fear. The most common type is atychiphobia, or fear of failure.

In a blog that came out (appropriately) in the Halloween season, the social productivity company Linkagoal published the results of a survey on what scares us most. In their Fear Factor Index poll, 31 percent of respondents said they feared failure. As they noted in a blog

## Five Signs the Fear of Failure Is Keeping You from Your Best Life

Left unchecked, the fear of failure will keep us from reaching our fullest potential. So it's important to know if, in either a big way or a small way, we're experiencing this kind of fear.

Here are five signs the fear of failure may be affecting you:

1. *You procrastinate or routinely avoid responsibility.* The more anxiety or fear you feel about reaching a goal, the more likely you are to delay action toward achieving it.

2. *You don't take charge of your own future.* When the fear of failure is present, initiative wanes. It becomes easier to accept whatever happens to you than to take the risk of crafting your own future around your goals, dreams, and potential.

3. *You set low expectations for yourself.* People who fear failure routinely set a low bar for themselves, hoping that a lower expectation will reduce their feelings of failure. Of course, at the same time, it also reduces their accomplishments and potential.

4. *You doubt yourself.* Nobody is perfectly capable of everything. But if the people around you believe in you and tell you that you can accomplish something, and yet you doubt yourself to the point of never trying, the fear of failure is holding you back.

5. *Your fear results in physical ailments.* Stress and anxiety can have many causes. If you suffer from frequent headaches, stomachaches, panic attacks, or other stress-induced ailments around new or challenging goals, they may be arising from a fear of failure.

post on the results, "When it comes to goal achievement, a fear [of] failing was a prominent reason why nearly half [of respondents] didn't achieve a goal at all or attempted to give it another try. 49% of applicable respondents said the fear of failure was a major setback, with fear of embarrassment (44%) and fear of it being too hard to achieve (43%) next in line."[1]

I've seen the fear of failure distract many people from life-changing pursuits.

I have a friend, David, who is a successful journalist. And like many journalists, he's long had a secret desire to write a novel. But he kept putting it off and putting it off. He told himself, *I need to build up some savings, because writing a novel is time consuming and may never pay a dollar.* That was true. But it also became an excuse.

He had a version of atychiphobia. *What if I write the novel and it's no good and nobody reads it?* he wondered. If that happened, David would no longer be able to tell himself, *I have the potential to write a great story.* Because if he'd given it his best and failed, a part of his self-perception would be disproved. A dream he had cherished for a long time would be dashed.

But as time went on, it became harder and harder for David to convince himself that there was plenty of time to fulfill his dream. By middle age, he was a successful journalist but had never written a word of fiction. If the potential was ever going to become actual, it had to start sometime. Besides, he was starting to feel bad about himself, like he was a coward.

David finally decided the possibility of never writing the book was worse than writing it and seeing it flop. He's writing his novel today. Will it sell? And if so, how many stars will reviewers give it? He doesn't know, and I don't know. But I admire my friend for trying. He already feels better about himself because he overcame his fears.

My friend David would tell you that he regrets not starting to write fiction twenty years ago. But then, due to fear, some people *never* get started living for things that matter.

A lot of people have one or more fears that combine to hold them back from pursuing goals they would like to achieve. Goals like these:

- starting a business
- moving to a different state
- changing careers
- asking for a promotion or raise
- looking for a new job
- leading a group
- initiating a friendship
- joining a club
- hosting a neighborhood get-together
- joining a gym

I can think of a lot of people who want to do things like this but they let fears and anxieties prevent them. What is fear holding *you* back from?

## Fears That Keep Us from Trying *Again*

Sometimes fear holds us back not from starting but from trying again. Overcoming fear is not a onetime achievement but a lifelong skill. Your first attempt (or second or third) at pursuing something mean-ingful may not go as well as you would've liked, but if you're ever going to be successful at it, you'll have to try again.

Even if you're successful, success brings its own challenges that can be anxiety inducing. What if, for example, your project has succeeded to a point where the next natural step is for you to do public speaking? To some people, public speaking is actually more intimidating than the thought of death. Or what if you might lose some privacy? Or what if you're tempted by power? These are fears of success, not fears of failure.

Linkagoal's research shows how fear can spoil the "try, try again" spirit, whatever the reason our progress has stalled. The Fear Factor

Index indicated that the top three fears that prevent people from trying to achieve a goal a second time include fear of failure (43 percent), fear of being too old (37 percent), and fear of lack of support from family and friends (37 percent).[2]

We're not a culture that admits failure, especially in an era of Photoshop and filtered social media clips. We love to trumpet our successes, but only a rare few openly discuss their failures—and usually it's in a context of how they ultimately succeeded. But everybody deals with failure in some way or another. If you have tried and failed, you're in good—and wide—company. What separates those without regret from those with regret is how they respond to failure.

An unpublished author named Joanne wrote a kids' book that she believed in. Unfortunately, publishers weren't so sure about it—a dozen of them rejected her manuscript. Joanne pinned her first rejection letter on the kitchen wall to motivate herself to keep going. And she did keep going, until a publisher finally took a chance on her.

We know this author as J. K. Rowling. Her Harry Potter series became the young-adult publishing phenomenon of modern times.[3]

A basketball player once stated in a television ad, "I've missed more than nine thousand shots in my career. I've lost almost three hundred games. Twenty-six times, I've been trusted to take the game-winning shot—and missed. I've failed over and over and over again in my life. And that is why I succeed."[4]

Succeed he did. According to ESPN, Michael Jordan was the greatest NBA player of all time.[5]

You may be thinking, *Well, these stories don't apply to me. I'm not J. K. Rowling or Michael Jordan.* And that's true. You're probably never going to be an author who can afford to live on a Scottish country estate or a basketball star with an athletic shoe named after you. But you don't need to be. You have a purpose and a good that you are designed to bring into this world. Allowing fear to keep you from it would be an unspeakable shame.

> You have a purpose and a good
> that you are designed to bring
> into this world.

These kinds of celebrity stories are often told to motivate others to keep going and not give up. But there's a more basic message in them for us. Before we can keep going, we've got to *overcome the fear that would cause us to give up.*

## His Own Saboteur

Randy is in his midforties, short and stocky, with a dark, close-cut beard. He's a family man and a product development manager. He works hard and supports his family, but he'd be the first to admit he's not accomplishing the fullest work he feels called to accomplish. He even confided in me recently that he deals with fear of failure every day of his life and that it has sabotaged every good job he's ever had— not because his fear keeps him from trying, but because it keeps him from fully succeeding.

"As a young boy, I was told constantly that I was a good-for-nothing and would never accomplish anything meaningful in life," he told me. "And it doesn't matter where life takes me or how much I succeed, I can't shake those words spoken over me by the people I loved the most. In my mind, it's only just a matter of time before I mess it all up."

He went on to explain how success in his career did not eliminate those beliefs; it seemed to magnify them.

"It didn't matter how far I progressed in a company, and it didn't matter how many kind words were delivered to me by my boss. I believed in my deepest heart that I was good for nothing. Even when everything was going great and I was excelling in my work, I lived in constant fear that my employer would eventually find out I was good for nothing. Because of that fear, I often turned down opportunities to grow or expand in the company. It seems like the higher I climbed, the more afraid I was of being found out. Eventually, in every position I've ever held, I'd resign and go somewhere else to start over. I was so afraid of being found out."

Randy's fear of failure (because of the messages that were delivered to him as a child) has kept him from fully succeeding in a role he is perfectly designed to fulfill. "It haunts me every day," he said. "I've left every wonderful job I've ever held. Not because I couldn't do it, but because of fear." My good friend's story illustrates how the fear of failure can distract us from our fullest potential, even if we manage to get started on a goal.

---

### The distraction of fear may be holding you back in significant ways from your fullest potential.

---

Make no mistake—the distraction of fear may be holding you back in significant ways from your fullest potential. Meanwhile, those closest to you need you to succeed.

## How Fear of Failure Blocks Your Progress

Fear of failure affects us at three points: when we're starting, when we're trying again after a failure, and when we're progressing. (That last one was Randy's downfall.)

Theo Tsaousides, a neuropsychologist and author of *Brainblocks,* said that in the short run, fear of failure influences the types of goals we pursue and how we go about trying to achieve them. For example, people with fear of failure may . . .

- focus their efforts more on preventing losses than on achieving gains
- avoid situations in which they expect to be evaluated or judged
- set lower standards for themselves
- create obstacles to undermine their own efforts to achieve their goals so that later they can blame the obstacles

Those are just the short-term consequences of fear of failure. If we let our fear of failure continue, it can do more than prevent some achievements; it can actually have debilitating effects on the kind of person we're becoming.

Tsaousides said,

> In the long-run, fear of failure could cause even bigger problems that affect a person's physical and mental health. People with fear of failure often experience fatigue and low energy, they feel emotionally drained, they are more dissatisfied with their lives, they experience chronic worry and hopelessness, and their performance in the relevant domains becomes objectively worse.[6]

## Name Them

Are you nodding your head at these words about how fear can distract you from your potential and purpose? What are your fears? By now you know I'm not talking about your fear of tight places, the sight of blood, or heights. What fears are holding you back from fulfilling your greatest potential and giving your best to the world?

It's not good enough to merely acknowledge that you have fears. If you want to cut them down to size, subvert them, and ultimately blow past them, you have to name them.

I'll go first.

At this point in my life, one fear that I worry might be holding me back from accomplishing things that matter is the fear of discomfort. Let me explain.

To be honest, I've got a comfortable life. I'm not talking about the stuff I own, because obviously as a minimalist I don't own a lot of stuff. What's more important to me is that I control my own schedule and the parameters of my work. I decide how many hours I'll work and on what. I decide who I'll meet with and when. My time and choices are my own. Hey, it's nice. Why would I want to mess that up?

For some people, being able to control their own schedule is the ultimate success symbol. But I see it differently.

One reason might be that there's something more important than my comfort.

Recently, my wife, Kim, and I were asked to provide marital counseling for couples going through conflict that threatens their marriages. Kim felt it was important that we follow through with the opportunity. Our marriage is healthy, and after being a pastor for so many years, I understand the importance of helping couples build strong marriages, but almost immediately, I resisted the idea.

Eventually, I stepped back and asked myself *why* I had reacted that way. The answer was that doing marital counseling would take up a lot of my free time and plunge me into other people's messes. Helping people doesn't always mean they stay on your desired schedule, and there's nothing comfortable about that. My fear of discomfort may, unfortunately, be keeping me from doing important things.

As we've seen from the Fear Factor Index, the fear of failure is the most common fear preventing people from doing things that matter. But a lot of other fears can come into play. Own yours. They may include:

- fear of rejection
- fear of the unknown
- fear of inadequacy
- fear of losing what you have
- fear of missing out
- fear of change
- fear of losing control (that's me)
- fear of discomfort (also me)
- fear of being yourself
- fear of not succeeding
- fear of being judged or ridiculed
- fear of getting hurt
- fear of leadership
- fear of exposure or loss of privacy
- fear of success

That's a lot of fears, and it's not even an exhaustive list.

To give you a little encouragement at this point, let me inform you that about 85 to 90 percent of the things people worry about never happen. And that's not opinion—that's fact! And even when worries do come true, the outcome is often better than we'd expected.[7] In other words, the potential reward is usually worth the risk—especially when it comes to accomplishing things that matter.

Also, in my experience, facing and overcoming fear builds courage over time. A fear that once looked like a mountain looming before us looks like a speed bump as we turn around and look back at it. As a result, we're more confident about conquering the even bigger mountain that stands before us now.

When therapists treat fear problems, many times they encourage something called habituation. It's a process of gradual, repeated exposure to something you fear. In this way, eventually, the thing becomes more familiar and the fear becomes manageable. It works the other way too. If we continually avoid things that cause us fear, the fear grows worse and more generalized.[8]

So let's face our fears, knowing that it won't be easy and that after we conquer one fear, another may lie beyond. But at least we're moving! Let me reframe your thinking about fear to make progress easier.

## Priorities in Fear

In his books, twentieth-century cultural anthropologist Ernest Becker (no relation to me) weaved together a philosophy arguing that most of a person's actions are based on his or her fear of death. But for Becker, it is not physical death that people fear. He contended that humanity's greatest fear is actually to die without one's life having mattered. He said, "What man really fears is not so much extinction, but extinction *with insignificance*. Man wants to know that his life has somehow counted, if not for himself, then at least in a larger scheme of things, that it has left a trace, a trace that has meaning."[9] I believe this is absolutely true.

This fear, however, may not be as immediate and obvious to us as other fears, like the fear of failure. You might think, *Who is ever going to know if I don't reach my full potential? On the other hand, everyone will notice if I fail today.* But *you* will notice. *You* may get to the end of your life and regret the chances you never took.

The point of *Things That Matter* is that we focus on this "fear of death with insignificance" and respond appropriately. Fear of death with insignificance is a good fear if it compels us to meaningful pursuits. And the more we mature, the more we feel its weight.

So, wherever you are in pursuing your goals, and whatever kind of fear you may be facing, I've got the same piece of advice for you. Visualize what it would be like to get to the end of life without ever fulfilling your potential. Now *that's* scary! You should be shaking in your boots about that possibility. Actually, we all should be shaking in our boots that you might give in to your fear, because we all need you and your greatest possible contribution to the world.

This visualization exercise can change your perspective. You'll think less about the fears that are keeping you from moving ahead and more about the totally legitimate, much more serious fear of going through life and never accomplishing the things you care about.

Fear this: wasting your life.

When your fear of not achieving your purposes is greater than your fear of trying, you'll begin to overcome the distraction of fear.

## Her Greatest Fear

One person who understands this trade-off is a young British woman named Melanie Kirk. She shared her story in an article titled "My Greatest Fear in Life." What is that fear? It's *not doing anything meaningful with her life.* She said that she doesn't want to get to the end of life and think she hadn't made the most of her days.

Melanie earned a university degree but decided she hated the field she chose, so upon graduating, she vowed never to work in a job that made her feel trapped. And she's kept that vow, spending her working hours on things she believes in, such as organic farming.

Recently, a relative of hers who was younger than her suddenly died. It reminded Melanie that a long life is no guarantee. There's only limited time to do what she wants to do.

So she's made another vow:

> A vow to live every day as if it's my one and only chance
> to make a mark, because IT IS.
> To live my life on purpose.
> To stop wasting time on things that don't matter.
> To step out of my comfort zone.
> To live with passion and courage of my convictions.
> To let go of the "what if's."
> To never, ever give up even when things get tough.
> Because at the end of the day life is far too precious a
> gift to squander.[10]

Read her manifesto again . . . slowly. Which of those vows do you disagree with? Isn't she describing the life we all want to live? Imagine how the world would change if we all made similar commitments. Imagine how your life would change.

## Cutting Fear Down to Size

Sometimes when we look at people who are accomplishing meaningful work, we think, *Well, it comes easy for them.* I don't think that's true. Instead, I believe most—*nearly all*—successful people had fears to overcome along the way to becoming who they are. If you have a role model or mentor in your life, ask her or him about it. I think you'll find that this person has had to deal with (and is probably still dealing with) fear. Almost every human being has fears and self-doubts, worries and anxieties. Yet they face the fear. And they find it manageable.

I started my *Becoming Minimalist* blog the very first week I started minimizing, in 2008. At that time I was a pastor, and I *loved* pastoring. I thought I'd do it for the rest of my life. Yet the *Becoming Minimalist* readership kept growing and growing. Through the blog, I was just trying to share my story and help as many people as I could, but the response far exceeded my expectations. I began to wonder, *Should I do this full time? After all, there are lots of pastors better than me in the ministry but not many people who seem to be better at inspiring others to own less.* Following a lot of thought and some encouragement from Kim and from close friends, I decided to make the leap.

Some might think my transition to full-time blogging was an easy, no-brainer step. The truth is, it was an anguishing three-and-a-half-year process for me. I was afraid every day leading up to the transition. And every day since, I've lived in fear that the whole thing is going to come tumbling down.

Let me tell you about the time I made my seven-year-old daughter burst into tears. It's not a story I'm proud of, but it goes to show how fear can grip everyone—even the person writing this chapter on overcoming it.

During dinner one evening, our daughter, Alexa, and son, Salem (four years older), were talking about their school lunches. Like kids everywhere, it seems, they weren't keen on the selections offered by the school cafeteria.

I joked, "Well, you better learn to like it. If this blogging thing doesn't work, you might have to put an extra lunch in your backpack for all of us to share for dinner."

I thought it was kind of funny, but . . .

Alexa started to cry.

Then Salem silently left the table.

Later, my wife said, "Joshua, maybe you shouldn't say things like that in front of the kids." That was an understatement. In fact, this scene was the culmination of countless little jokes and quips I'd made over the previous two years about not making it as a blogger. It was only at this dinner that I realized how much it had been affecting our kids. Salem and Alexa were genuinely afraid that the breadwinner in the family—me—wasn't going to be winning much bread anymore. And then how would we make it as a family?

The thing is, Salem and Alexa weren't the only ones who were scared. Kim and I were nervous about our financial future as well, me especially. I'd identified a goal—creating a new career based on promoting simple living over the internet—and I was prepared to pursue it because I thought it was important. But it came with risks. Maybe this minimalism blogging thing was only suitable as a sideline. Maybe it wasn't something I could devote all my working hours to while supporting a family. I had always worked for stable organizations that gave me a paycheck every two weeks, and I was going to give that up. Not to mention, what if I was a terrible boss of myself?

I was so concerned about the financial risks that I took the transition to full-time minimalism blogging very slowly. For a year and a half, I debated the possibility but approached it as only a spare-time project while working at a church in Vermont. Then I took another church job in Arizona, because the Vermont job was designed to come to an end in two years. By that point, according to the plan, I would take *Becoming Minimalist* to the next level and rely on it as my wage source.

And that's the way it played out.

Looking back, the fears I dwelt upon over that three-and-a-half-year transition process seem a little silly. I've said that our mountainous fears can look like speed bumps in retrospect, and this was one of those situations. The financial side of my minimalism gig has worked out fine, and my kids have never needed to steal lunches from school.

I'll share a few more details of how I took small, but real, steps to overcome my fear.

When I went full time with *Becoming Minimalist*, I was making $2,000 a month online. Kim and I determined that our family of four needed $4,000 a month to live on, covering things like the mortgage and health insurance (but not including vacations or nonnecessities— thank you, minimalism). At the time, we had almost $18,000 in the bank that we had saved through hard work over the course of three years, or a nine-month cushion where we could cover the $2,000 monthly shortfall.

I told myself that if we hadn't become self-supporting through *Becoming Minimalist* within nine months, I would know I wasn't supposed to be doing this as a career. A decade later, I'm still doing it, and I couldn't be happier. I believe this is my calling and purpose, and I don't regret the decision for a single moment, even though it was incredibly difficult at the time.

Of course, it's easier to overcome your fear of failing to launch a new enterprise that matters to you if you have a safety net—financial, relational, or whatever kind of security it may be. It's great to know you could always go live with your in-laws for a while if the new business fails. Or that there are some retirement savings you could draw on early if you needed to. Or that you could get your old job back. It can take some of the fear out of trying.

Overcoming fear isn't about making unwise decisions. Put a safety net in position if you need to. But what I'm saying is, be self-aware and intentional while doing it. There's a difference between being held back because you're truly not ready or the timing isn't right and being held back by fear. A desire for security can be motivated by fear. Prudence can become an excuse for procrastination.

By all means, be wise. Count the cost before you start to build your new future or make a major life change. But don't let insecurity hold you back when it's time to try. We need your biggest contribution to the world that you can possibly give. *You* need your biggest contribution that you can possibly give.

## Number of Lives You Have to Invest in for Great Good: One

Fear and desire are closely related emotions. For example, if you fear hunger, you will desire wealth. If you fear change, you will desire stability. If you fear loneliness, you will desire relationship. If you fear failure, you will desire comfort. And the list continues.

Not every fear is wrong, but every fear does result in an opposing desire. We can never eliminate fear, but we can prioritize fears so that our fear of not living up to our fullest potential outweighs whatever fears keep us from taking action and making a difference. That's courage: action taken not in the absence of fear but in the face of fear. Or, in the immortal words of the Great Wizard of Oz, "True courage is in facing danger when you are afraid, and that kind of courage you have in plenty."[11]

> # Courage: action taken not in the absence of fear but in the face of fear.

So let me ask you in closing, before moving on to the external distractions that keep us from a meaningful life: If you lived your entire life and never took a risk, do you think you would regret it? Probably so.

Fear has a pernicious way of distracting us and keeping us from pursuing our goals, reaching our fullest potential, and bringing our best to the world. You don't want to be like Jiao (the longtime perfume saleswoman) and countless other people who regret never having tried to do something more significant and rewarding with their lives.

If fear is keeping you from purposefully living the life you've always desired, try discovering your hidden fears and intentionally redirecting them. For starters, fear the thought of wasting the only life you've got.

# 4

## Wounded

### *Overcoming the Distraction of Past Mistakes*

There is always tension between the possibilities we aspire
to and our wounded memories and past mistakes.

—Seán Brady

Deanna Hutchison is a successful blogger and speaker. She's at peace
with her God, excited about her new marriage, and fulfilled by her
work. For a long time, though, it looked like mistakes made in her
past could cost her everything, including her life.

In her case, as in so many others', her troubles traced all the way
back to her childhood. She grew up in a two-parent home, with her
dad working as a salesman and her mother staying home. Deanna's
mother was nurturing. Her father, however, was at work much of the
time, and when he came home, he was often feeling stressed by what
went on at his job. He loved Deanna but had a temper, so he came off
to Deanna as a rage-filled disciplinarian. She lacked emotional security.

Looking back on her younger adult years, she told me, "My mind
was filled with lots of negative self-talk and even lies. I never thought
I was good enough. I thought I was unworthy and would mess things
up. Those tapes played over and over in my head well past childhood.
I literally thought I was stupid."

As a result of her damaged thinking, Deanna looked for self-worth in a host of things outside herself. She got into drinking, drug use, and relationships with men who weren't good for her. By the time she was in her thirties, Deanna was an alcoholic and a drug addict, and her future seemed to be closing down.

Growing up, she'd wanted to get married and have five children, but she was beginning to doubt that would ever happen. She'd also wanted to be a teacher. And in fact, she'd been a high school math teacher for a while—until she'd had to give it up because of her addictions. Finally she was alone, depressed, and deeply in debt. She was convinced she would either die or go insane if things didn't change soon.

She started evaluating how she'd gotten to this point. *How did I end up a full-blown addict in my thirties?* she asked herself. *Why did I allow myself to be treated so harshly by men? And what happened to that little girl who had a big ol' bucket full of dreams?* She decided she would do whatever it took to find out.

For her, the problems stemmed from her relationship with her father, and as she would say, the turning point came when she got right with God. Other people go through other kinds of turning points in life when they begin to put the damage of their pasts behind them, but Deanna's turning point was primarily spiritual.

In 2009, at the age of thirty-six, Deanna began doing the hard work of addiction recovery and getting her finances and work life together. She still has challenges stemming from the past, but her life is full of victories too.

She offers a warning for all of us. "If we don't identify ways in our past where we developed unhealthy coping skills, find the courage to heal and forgive, and learn new coping mechanisms, we all can be subject to reacting out of the wounds of our past."[1]

## Mistakes Committed and Mistakes Suffered

Deanna is right. In our pursuit of the things that matter to us, past mistakes can be a drag, a distraction, and a deterrent from moving ahead. By "past mistakes," I'm talking about anything negative you've done or that has been done to you that is preventing you from making progress or achieving accomplishments. Sometimes "mistakes" isn't a strong enough word, as in cases of child abuse. Sometimes the actions in question are downright evil. Regardless, big or little, committed by us or by someone else, past mistakes have a hobbling effect on many of us.

All of us, in one way or another, are influenced by troubles in our pasts. In many cases, a previous mistake or hardship can be like a hand reaching out and grabbing us around the ankle to hold us back. To make this distraction even more difficult to overcome, often it's not just one problem but a combination of errors and mistreatment that accounts for what's gone wrong in our lives. We feel shame and guilt.

Although some past mistakes are easily forgettable, others are powerful and have a long-term effect. They can prevent us from having the vision to do things that matter in the first place. They can contribute to some of the fears we discussed in the last chapter. Or they can dog us and hinder us as we try to pursue our life goals. I call them a *distraction,* but sometimes they look more like a *derailment*—something that makes a train wreck out of a life. In the end, we may regret the opportunities and possibilities we missed because of them.

When we should embrace change, past mistakes make us hesitant.

When we should be bold, past mistakes make us anxious.

When we should believe in ourselves, past mistakes make us feel unworthy.

When we should dream big, past mistakes cause us to think small.

When we should say yes, past mistakes convince us that all we've got is a no.

So many people waste time brooding over past mistakes or disqualifying themselves because of them. If you want to know why many people never get around to doing the things that matter to them, one of the most common reasons is right here. And how about you? As I describe in more depth what past mistakes look like, be thinking about the past events or patterns that have set the course most strongly for you.

Past mistakes come in different shapes and sizes. It's also important to note that while some people might see something as a mistake in their life, others may not define it as such or may have turned it around in their life to the point that they wouldn't even call it a mistake anymore.

But for the sake of framing this chapter, here are some of the mistakes that may derail a person's life:

- dropping out of school
- a foolish business venture
- going bankrupt
- unfaithfulness in marriage
- ill treatment toward another person
- an accident that harmed another person
- embarrassing yourself in public
- losing your temper with your child and alienating him or her
- committing a crime that's going to be on your record for all time

And it's not just onetime mistakes either. Sometimes it's patterns—bad habits, addictions, negative dispositions—that are so ingrained they seem to be an irremovable part of your nature. For example, maybe . . .

- You're in AA and off the stuff for now, but you well remember that you've had to reset your sobriety clock before.

- You're socially awkward and not good with people.
- You're chronically disorganized, messy, and inefficient.
- You can't seem to get out of the debt trap.
- You have a track record of sabotaging yourself.
- You keep poor boundaries and get taken advantage of over and over.
- You're indecisive.
- You're a perfectionist.
- You're fearful and defeatist.

Then there are the presumptions we make about our ability to change. As we've been looking at life goals so far in this book, have you said or thought any of these?

- "I never know where to start."
- "It's too late."
- "I'm too old."
- "I don't have what it takes."
- "I've never done anything like this before."
- "Small goals are good enough for me."
- "I'm not a leader."
- "I don't have the right education [or right experience, right credentials, etc.]."
- "Oh, I could never . . ."

Last, and possibly most painful, is the harm done to you by nature or by other people. For Deanna Hutchison, it was her father's temper that set her on a downward course. Other kinds of "mistakes" that affect us but that we're not responsible for can include losses, offenses, betrayals, even crimes and disasters.

As you look ahead to pursuing your goals, do you need to consider any of these?

- a disability
- abandonment or neglect
- chronic illness
- verbal, sexual, or physical abuse
- racist treatment
- loss of a loved one

Let me assure you that I'm not taking any of these categories of past mistakes lightly. But so many times, people get stuck because of mistakes—rather than facing and overcoming them—and are unable to move on. If we wait to be healthy, perfect, and prepared in every way, we'll never accomplish anything. Everything valuable that has ever been done was done by someone with flaws and wounds. Some greater, some lesser, for sure. But there are no perfect people.

---

If we wait to be healthy, perfect, and prepared in every way, we'll never accomplish anything. Everything valuable that has ever been done was done by someone with flaws and wounds.

---

## Bouncing Back

How prevalent is this distraction in people's lives? In our Things That Matter Survey, we asked, "How much do your past mistakes hold you back from achieving the future you'd like to have?" A clear majority—61 percent of respondents—said their own past mistakes held them back "somewhat" to "very much."

Do your past mistakes hold you back from achieving the future you'd like to have?

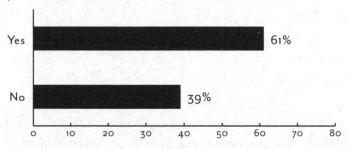

Additionally, we asked, "How much do wrongs committed against you in the past hold you back from achieving the future you'd like to have?" Here, over half of respondents—55 percent—said "somewhat" to "very much."

That's a lot of potential being bottled up. How sad! Almost two out of every three people say that their past, in one way or another, is holding them back from the future they'd like to have. My heart aches for every single one of us. Not just those who feel held back but also those who could be benefiting from us walking in wholeness and victory.

Is there hope that we can release ourselves from the hold that past

Do wrongs committed against you in the past hold you back from achieving the future you'd like to have?

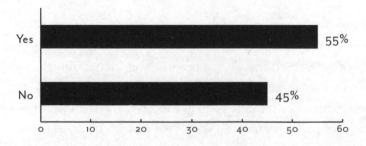

mistakes have on us? There's more than hope. Innumerable examples show us that we *can* rise above the destruction in our pasts. This is not a new distraction that keeps people from things that matter; it is as old as humanity itself.

Back in 1962, Victor and Mildred Goertzel wrote a book called *Cradles of Eminence,* in which they investigated the life stories of more than four hundred high-achieving people, including Louis Armstrong, Frida Kahlo, Eleanor Roosevelt, and Henry Ford. The book is still cited today for its key findings: 75 percent of the Goertzels' subjects "had grown up in a family burdened by a severe problem: poverty, abuse, absent parents, alcoholism, serious illness or some other misfortune."[2]

Fifty-five years after the Goertzels' book came out, *Wall Street Journal* contributor Meg Jay wrote, "If the Goertzels were to repeat their study today, they would find many more examples of women and men who rose to great heights after difficult childhoods—Oprah Winfrey, Howard Schultz, LeBron James and Sonia Sotomayor, to name just a few. Today, we often use the word 'resilient' to describe such people."[3]

Resilience. Determination. Being a fighter. That's what Jay said explains the difference between those who triumph over early hardship and those who do not.

Maybe you're tired of hearing words like those. Maybe you're tired of fighting. But you need to hear this. We need you to be a fighter. We need you to show up in your own life, regardless of the hurts of your past. The potential inside you can be bottled up no longer.

And there is only one way to learn resilience: "Overcoming childhood adversity is a phenomenal struggle indeed. It is a heroic, powerful, perilous, often decadeslong endeavor, yet one that, over time, can lead to both ordinary and extraordinary success."[4]

**Move past the past.**

You can't change the past—but you can loosen the grip it has on you. And maybe the pain from your past will even make you better at doing meaningful things than you ever could have been without it.

## Your Signpost

I knew a successful corporate executive who used to say to me, "Great leaders run toward problems." That's good advice not just for leaders dealing with organizational dysfunction but also for all of us dealing with our own problems. Too many times, we're tempted to deny, ignore, or hide from our problems. That's why guilt and shame from our pasts can have such a high level of influence on our lives that they prevent us from pursuing the things that would make our lives more complete today.

Let's run *toward* our problems. Let's face them. And let's do something about them.

> Let's run *toward* our problems.
> Let's face them. And let's do
> something about them.

You may feel that you have already dealt with past mistakes, but if they're still holding you back, that's a sign that they are affecting you more powerfully than they need to. I urge you to create your own turning point with regard to past mistakes. Plant a signpost that you can look back at and say to yourself, *That's where I turned things around.* Once you put errors and pain in your rearview mirror, you'll find you are freer to move on to the destinations you've picked out for yourself.

*If you've done harm to others . . .*

1. Acknowledge to yourself what you did and the harm it caused others. Try to identify why you did it, what this says about your weaknesses, and what you may still need to work on in yourself.
2. Allow yourself to feel remorse and regret.
3. If you're a believer in God, you may wish to seek his forgiveness. Remind yourself that if God forgives you, you are free to forgive yourself.
4. Apologize to those you hurt and ask their forgiveness, if that's possible and wouldn't make things worse. If the person you hurt is no longer around, you might find it helpful to speak the apology aloud in an empty room or write a letter. You did what you could to apologize.
5. If possible, make amends to the person you hurt. If that's not possible, is there some way you could "pay it forward" by doing a good deed for someone else? This action will help solidify the planting of that signpost as a turning point.
6. Tell yourself, *My mistake was wrong and harmful, but it's over. It's in the past now. I've moved beyond it, and it won't stop me from living a better life in the future.* Repeat as often as necessary.

*If harm has been done to you . . .*

1. Acknowledge the harm and what it did to you. Identify who (if anyone) is responsible.
2. If people are responsible for this harm, forgive them. This is not to excuse or minimize their behavior. It is to release them from the ill will you've been holding against them in your heart. This is for your own good. You can forgive even if the other people don't admit guilt and even if the other people never know about it.
3. If the harm done to you comes from nature or fate (such as a dis-

ability or a natural disaster), there is no one to forgive. Instead, you must accept it. Don't deny what happened, and don't blame yourself or anyone else. It just is. You don't need to play it down or blow it out of proportion.

4. Tell yourself, *What happened to me was bad and harmful. But I've let go of my anger about it, and I will not let it stop me from living a better life in the future.*

Disclaimer: In many cases, even when we make a decisive break from past mistakes, we still have to endure lingering negative consequences. But those consequences no longer need to be *controlling* us. We've found a way to escape the grasp that past harm can keep us in.

No matter your past or personality, you can (and should) overcome a defeatist attitude toward life. At some point, if we don't overcome this thinking, we allow the mistakes of our pasts to sabotage our presents and our futures to a degree that helps no one.

---

## No one is so guilty or so damaged that they can't make something different of their future and do something that is meaningful in the world.

---

I truly believe that no one is so guilty or so damaged that they can't make something different of their future and do something that is meaningful in the world. One reason I'm so confident about this is that what was destructive can actually be redeemed and made constructive. It's not easy work, but it is worth it.

## When Should You Seek Professional Help?

Christine Wilkens, a national certified counselor and trauma professional, offered these questions to help determine if you should seek professional help:

- Did I suffer wrongs committed against me in childhood (prior to puberty), a period of critical brain development?
- Have I experienced anything that caused me to fear for my life or for the lives of those close to me?
- Am I constantly ruminating or thinking about a past trauma or mistake?
- Am I never satisfied in life? Do I have trouble relaxing?
- Am I unable to maintain relationships?
- Do I feel people don't take enough time for me? Am I constantly feeling dismissed?
- Do I feel the need to constantly reinvent myself?
  Have I ever been treated for anxiety disorder or depression in the past, and do I wonder if I need a reevaluation?
- Do I have a treatment plan but frequently fail to stick with it?
- Do I always find myself avoiding plans for success in life?

Christine said that if you answered yes to any of these questions and you're curious whether your life could get better, she recommends you talk with a licensed therapist to see if counseling or other treatment might be right for you.[5]

## Overcomer

From an early age, Jada Reid's life has been about overcoming. Sometimes it has been about proving herself to others. Sometimes it has been because she had no other choice.

When Jada was five, she was surrendered to the state by her single mother, who could no longer care for her and her siblings. Jada was placed in the New York State foster care system. During the next eight years, Jada lived in several homes with unhealthy relationships and was sexually abused.

Eventually Jada went back to living with her mother, but by then she had been scarred by neglect and mistreatment. "I tried to overcome my past by becoming a perfectionist," she shared with me. Through hard work, she became a top student as well as a high school track star. Then she joined the military, where she continued to be motivated by excelling.

After her military service, Jada had to overcome both gender and racial obstacles to join the ranks of law enforcement. "Anytime I was told I couldn't do something," she said, "I wanted to do it all the more."

But her desire to achieve eventually took a negative spin. As she witnessed other law enforcement officers enriching themselves corruptly, she wanted in on the action. She resigned from the force and began dealing both drugs and guns. "I was good at it," she recalled. "I bought my mom a house with the money. I became very materialistic, buying gold and diamonds and anything I could purchase to finally show off my 'success.'"

Her journey moved from dealing to addiction. Eventually her life choices caught up with her, and she went to prison three times. On her third stay, rather than gaming the system to get out early, she decided she would serve her entire sentence. There, she went through a personal transformation in which she offered forgiveness to those who had wronged her and received redemption for herself. "That was the day my mindset about myself changed. It was the day I saw who I could become and the good I could bring into the world."

After prison, Jada moved to Arizona to begin her new life. After working a few jobs to pay the bills and get on her feet, she began seeking work in local nonprofit organizations as a means to give back and help others. With her record, it wasn't easy for her to qualify for a fingerprint clearance card, but an officer helped her get one. She had to own her past and make amends where necessary (she still had outstanding warrants in neighboring states).

She told me, "It was one of the most emotional days of my life, Joshua. The road has not been easy, and there have been a lot of ups and downs. But that fingerprint card that allowed me to work at nonprofit organizations in Arizona was a symbol that I had overcome my past and was living a new life."

Since then, she has dedicated her life to serving those in need, including the homeless and disadvantaged, even becoming a trusted resource in the Arizona public school system with a reputation for helping teens in poverty. It's all come full circle for Jada. Recently she moved back in with her elderly mother to care for her, and she now works at a home for troubled teens in New York, helping them avoid the mistakes she made.

## Redeeming the Past

While we're moving past the past like Jada Reid, let's have the courage to listen to our pain, because sometimes it can teach us where we need to work on ourselves. Sometimes it can help us get better at pursuing our goals. And in a surprising number of cases, we can actually find major life purposes in the midst of our pain.

Remember Deanna Hutchison, the woman whose dysfunctional relationship with her father in childhood led to so many problems as she grew up? One thing she had to work on as she finally recovered from substance abuse and self-destructive patterns was her financial debt. It took her three and a half years to dig herself out of the financial hole she'd created, but with resilience and determination, she did it. Then she went further. Having experienced firsthand how hard it was to repair finances while recovering from substance abuse, Deanna decided to help other women in the same position. "Everything I've been through has gained me the honor of helping other women in recovery," she said. Today, she works with recovering women who want to get better at money management and "mental wealth."

This is a pattern I see over and over. So many times, our harmful past experiences open our eyes to others who are hurting, give us hearts filled with compassion, or show us places where we can help.

Here's another example.

Emilia, a friend of mine, volunteers at a nonprofit that serves military veterans suffering from posttraumatic stress disorder. Many soldiers who have served in war zones bring back with them flashbacks, nightmares, anxiety, and mood changes that make reentry into society and reunion with their families rough. Emilia acts as a sponsor, advising newly returned vets in readjusting to their hometowns and family lives. Although not a veteran herself, she has a reputation for really understanding PTSD and for sticking with victims through an often lengthy recovery.

This volunteering gig is completely different from Emilia's day job as a real estate agent. I asked her how she got into her volunteering specialty.

"I used to be married," she said to me with a heavy heart. "His name was Daniel, and he returned from active duty with severe PTSD. He came back a different man than he was when he left. He struggled and worked so hard to readjust but just couldn't get over the trauma. It's like the PTSD overcame him and he became someone he never wanted to be. It began to spill over into our marriage, with abuse and turmoil, and the marriage had to end."

Emilia is a woman who has suffered tremendously because of untreated PTSD in a loved one—in fact, her entire life was shattered because of it. But instead of letting it bury her, she used it as a springboard to help other soldiers and their families affected by PTSD so that other women can be spared the pain she has felt. Emilia is living a life today she will never regret.

If you've been thinking that your past mistakes disqualify you from pursuing things that are meaningful or important to you, I want to flip your thinking there. It could be that those very circumstances *qualify* you to own a particular goal or good work. You can learn lessons that would be available to you in no other way. You can take your suffering and use it to ease someone else's suffering. And in this way, it's possible not only to escape the enslavement of the past but also to make it your servant in doing good things that truly matter.

I don't say every mistake turns into a mission. This distraction can't always become a destination. But we should at least be alert to the possibility. And when it *does* happen, the redemption that occurs is beautiful to observe.

## Finding Pride

Let's recall our purpose in pursuing things that matter. It's to get to the end of life with more satisfaction over how we spent our time on earth and fewer regrets about the choices we made. We can't expect to do this unless we deal with the distractions and regrets we've already stacked up. And I know that seems hard.

The reality is that we all face different mistakes, hurts, or predispositions from our past. They range from nuisances to trauma. Sometimes, as we begin to deal with and overcome them, there is a moment of realization about how much these past mistakes have kept us from pursuing the things we love. The thinking might sound like this: *I can't believe how much time and energy I've wasted because of my past. I feel ashamed of it. How do I overcome this guilt?*

Here's my answer: You overcome the guilt and shame by finding pride in the person you're becoming and the changes you're making today. Be joyful about what your life is going to look like.

You can't change the past, but you can move beyond it in hope of a better future. You can have more freedom to love, to serve, and to live the kind of life that doesn't result in regret.

---

## You can't change the past, but you can move beyond it in hope of a better future.

---

Move past the past. Create a turning point for yourself.

When the door of opportunity opens, past mistakes will still say, "Stop right there."

But now you can reply, "Not this time."

# PART 3

---

# DISTRACTIONS OF THE
# LESSER GOOD

# 5

## The Me Monster

### Overcoming the Distraction of Happiness

An individual has not started living until he can rise
above the narrow confines of his individualistic concerns
to the broader concerns of all humanity.

—MARTIN LUTHER KING JR.

The "pursuit of happiness" is famously enshrined in the United States
Declaration of Independence. Not that anybody was waiting for
Thomas Jefferson's permission to seek happiness for themselves—we
all naturally want to do it. And there's nothing wrong with that.

As long as it's the right kind of happiness. Otherwise it's just a distraction.

See, somewhere along the way (or maybe it's always been like this),
it appears we human beings confused the pursuit of happiness with
the pursuit of self. As a result, we think we'll be happiest if we focus
on ourselves, spend our resources on ourselves, and meet our own
needs and desires—sometimes even at the expense of others. We see
this all around us.

All you have to do is watch young children playing and observe
how they monopolize their favorite toys, and you'll know how human
it is to be selfish. Nobody has to teach a child not to share.

Now, most of us aren't absolutely selfish in our pursuit of happiness. We include our loved ones. Maybe a few other people too. But it's a pretty small list, with Me at the top.

Serving ourselves comes naturally for most of us—it always has. But when we try to satisfy our desire for happiness in the pursuit of self, we fall short of the truest, most lasting forms of happiness. The pursuit of selfish desires may offer some pleasure in the short run, but in the long term, the happiness is never lasting. Misplaced, the pursuit of happiness can become the distraction that keeps us from more meaningful pursuits.

The pursuit of self and the pursuit of lasting happiness are not the same. In fact, at times, they run completely opposite routes.

At the end of your life, would you be prouder of having spent years working and saving to buy a second home *or* in doing what you can to help the poor or suffering in your community? Would you find more pride in having spent most of your spare time with sports shows and video games *or* in doing the creative work that you were uniquely suited for?

The best, most direct pathway to lasting happiness and fulfillment is to look not only at your own interests but also at the interests of others. When we begin living our lives for the sake of others, our lives immediately take on greater value. We no longer live for the benefit of one or a few; we begin living for the benefit of many.

---

The best, most direct pathway to
lasting happiness and fulfillment
is to look not only at your own
interests but also at the interests
of others.

---

Psychiatrist and philosopher Viktor Frankl said, "Happiness . . . cannot be pursued; it must ensue, and it only does so as the unintended side-effect of one's personal dedication to a cause greater than oneself or as the by-product of one's surrender to a person other than oneself."[1]

Happiness can't be *pursued*. It must *ensue*.

Have you ever tried to hand-feed a wild bird? If you approach too rapidly or thrust the food toward it, it will fly away, scared of you. But if you're patient and appear not to be interested in the bird, it may slowly work its way to you.

Let's not pursue happiness. Let's pursue purpose . . . and allow happiness to come to us.

## Happiness Dead Ends

I am well aware that when I call into question the wisdom of a self-focused pursuit of happiness, I sound like a spoilsport, if not a crank. Our society seems fixated these days on the pursuit of happiness, and the most commonly announced path to arrive there is by looking out for oneself. It just seems to make so much sense that to be happy, we should pursue what looks like happiness to us. Countless people around us are living their lives just that way—and they sure seem to be happy. Consumerism is built on the principle that the pursuit of self is the key to happiness.

But the alternative viewpoint—that the best pathway to lasting happiness is found by looking out for the interests of others—is not simply a matter of my opinion. It has been proven in scientific studies on the matter.

Happiness studies (known as *positive psychology*) represent an entire field of inquiry on their own. Here we're just going to look at some representative evidence that supports the notion that the truest forms of happiness occur when we live for others.

First, let's look at *wealth.* Does accumulating lots of money and possessions offer a pathway to a state of happiness? Culture says yes. Science says no.

Researchers at the University of California, Berkeley, paired study participants with one another to play a game of Monopoly. This study had nothing to do with studying a player's skill in putting hotels on Park Place and Boardwalk and everything to do with seeing how winning the game would affect people. As business school professor Raj Raghunathan described it,

> The game was rigged so that one of the participants quickly became far wealthier than the other. The researchers then observed, through a one-way mirror, the participants' behaviors. It turned out that the wealthier a participant grew, the meaner he/she progressively became. For example, the wealthier participants started assuming more dominant postures and began talking down to their "poorer" counterparts. They also consumed a greater share of a bowl of pretzels meant to be shared equally.[2]

Raghunathan explained why these results are important: because they show us wealth tends to make people (a) *less generous* and (b) *more isolated.* And both generosity and relational connectedness are strongly associated with happiness.[3] Transferred to the real world, these results could explain why people can get richer and richer and sadder and sadder and never really understand what's going on.

Well, if riches can't be trusted to deliver happiness, what about *success* and *fame*? We live in a world of striving where people are always trying to "get ahead" at work and "get noticed" by the boss and others. How's that working for them? Again, science can tell us.

A study at the University of Rochester in New York evaluated the goals and happiness of 147 college graduates one year after graduation and then again a year after that. The results? "Those who had attained the wealth and fame goals were less happy . . . than those who achieved more intrinsic goals such as personal growth." The reason for this seems primarily to be that the high achievers felt they were living their lives in ways predetermined by others. Meanwhile, "those who focused on intrinsic goals such as personal growth, enduring relationships and helping in the community 'showed substantial increases in life satisfaction, well-being and happiness areas.'"[4]

Now let's make it more interesting. What about *sex*? Surely indulging in promiscuity makes people happy, doesn't it? At least, that's what our culture (seemingly every television series and movie) tells me.

Professor Marina Adshade summarized her findings in this area by pointing out that people with more sexual partners are less happy than people with one. And people who cheat on their partners are less happy than those who do not. "That's counterintuitive, muses Adshade, if one's first instinct might be to assume that since 'sex makes us happy' and 'variety is the spice of life, having more sexual partners must make us happier.'"[5] Yet the research she consulted unambiguously shows that promiscuity doesn't deliver the payout of happiness that those who indulge in it expect.[6] Why would that be? Is it because even sex is more satisfying in the long run when viewed selflessly?

Let's try once more, with *beauty*. Everyone wants to look good. Does focusing on one's own physical self-improvement deliver happiness?

Perhaps cosmetic surgery is as good an indicator here as anything. Increasing numbers of people are willing to hand over thousands of dollars and go through the anxiety and pain of surgery in order to get a medically unnecessary nose job or tummy tuck. Does this kind of physical reconstruction wind up making them feel better about themselves?

Apparently not. According to a *Psychology Today* article, plastic surgery "doesn't address fundamental issues of self-esteem," depression, or unhappiness.

> At least at younger ages, one large study found, cosmetic surgery patients are a more troubled group—and the procedure doesn't help. This study is important because it followed more than 1,500 teenage girls for 13 years, and the researchers didn't know who would actually have surgery in that time. The 78 girls who did were more likely to be anxious or depressed and had a greater increase in those symptoms over the period than non-patients.[7]

Wealth. Success. Fame. Sex. Beauty. It seems many of the self-centered pursuits of happiness fall short in their results.

We're going to have to look further.

## Embracing Servanthood

I want to make it clear that I'm not opposed to reasonable self-care. After all, you can't pour from an empty cup, as the old saying goes. We all should be giving proper attention to our own well-being and health and finding things we enjoy doing.

But there's a big difference between self-care and self-centeredness. Consistently making choices that are about me, me, me will never deliver the greatest levels of happiness, nor will it prevent regrets at the end of life. "Happiness" can become a distraction from more life-giving pursuits. For those, we need to set our sights higher—to the major life purposes we've identified.

What I've found most effective at reorienting people's focus from our own desires to others' needs is service. That is, instead of serving *ourselves,* we serve *others.*

This is because becoming unselfish is not an intellectual exercise—you don't just think yourself into unselfishness. It's not even an act, like writing a check to a charity or dropping off a box of unused goods at Goodwill, as valuable as those things may be. Unselfishness is a *quality* you acquire only when you go and do something for others. At first it may seem more intentional than natural, but over time, a genuine selflessness begins to emerge. The doing creates the being. You go from *choosing to serve* to *being a servant.*

The kind of service that brings about this transformation may not have anything to do with your major life purposes. The ultimate goal is to clear the distraction of self-centered happiness away so that you can more effectively achieve the things that matter to you, but to start with, *any* act of service can help to slay your monster of selfishness.

So do something that helps other people through personal involvement with them:

- visit a patient in a hospital
- serve a meal to the homeless
- listen to a friend who is troubled
- mentor a youth through Big Brothers Big Sisters
- babysit for stressed-out parents
- become a tutor in a school or after-school program
- be a Good Samaritan by helping a stranger change a flat tire

See a need around you? Meet it today. And the life you change just may be your own.

My advice to shrink your Me Monster is to just get out there and . . .

**Serve somebody.**

## The Smell Stays with Me

---

Back when I was a youth pastor, I visited Ecuador to do some service work with fifty high school students. During that week, we built a school, fixed up homes, and did other practical service projects.

One afternoon, the director of the nonprofit we were partnering with asked us all to pile in a bus, as we were going to do something different that day. We drove for quite a while, outside the city of Quito, and eventually pulled into one of the city's garbage dumps. This was not a well-maintained garbage dump like you'd expect to see in your local town. This was just an open field where garbage was dumped, above the ground, piled high as far as the eye could see.

When we arrived, our director explained to us, "Today we're going to feed the families and play with the children who live here." He went on to explain how hundreds of families made their living by going through the garbage dumped there each day, searching for anything they could use or sell. Sometimes they would make just pennies a day out of it.

That was over a decade ago, and I still recall that last step off the bus into this new world. I'll remember, until the day I die, the dirty faces of the children with their big round eyes and their malnourished bodies. I can still see the look of desperation on their parents' faces as they did whatever they could to survive. And I will never, ever forget the awful smell of that garbage dump, magnified by the rays of the beating sun, while I suddenly came to terms with the reality that this was their home.

This. This is an experience that could never be replicated by reading a book, visiting a website, or even writing a check. There are children today, all around the world, living in garbage dumps searching for food or aluminum cans to recycle. It's one thing to read about this reality and cognitively understand that it happens, but it's something entirely different to see it and smell it and hold the hands of the children. *This* is the effect that getting outside ourselves and helping another human being can have on us.

I will never be the same because of that one afternoon. And it came through simple acts of stepping into the needs of others and serving.

But you don't have to travel to a far-flung part of the world to get dirt under your fingernails by serving another.

## A Life of Goodness

Dion Mitchell grew up near Toledo, Ohio, in comfortable circumstances. In his childhood and youth, he did not often come into contact with poor people. Nor did Dion's family have a consistent pattern of serving the needy. But every Thanksgiving, for reasons he wasn't even able to articulate, they would deliver meals to poor families in their small town who were short on food.

When telling me about his experience, Dion did some quick calculations in his head. "I think we only did this for about six years, and it took maybe two hours each time. So that's twelve hours total out of my life. But do you know what, Joshua? Visiting those families on Thanksgiving is one of the most vivid memories I have of my childhood. Seeing how other people lived and knowing what it felt like to give helped prepare me for serving others in bigger ways when I was a grown-up."

Serving changes us.

Around the world or just around the block in our own hometowns, these simple acts of service that prompt change in our hearts don't have to be extravagant. Again, science shows us this.

Emily Esfahani Smith, author of *The Power of Meaning*, said in a *New York Times* op-ed, "The idea that a meaningful life must be or appear remarkable is not only elitist but also misguided. . . . The most meaningful lives, I've learned, are often not the extraordinary ones.

They're the ordinary ones lived with dignity." In her article, she cited two studies that show us that selfless living enhances our lives. One study discovered that adolescents' household chores can have significant implications on the teens' positive well-being as they contribute to something greater than themselves. The second study found that self-serving actions feel good when they are being carried out but do not support positive effects in the long run. Conversely, selfless action, even something as simple as cheering up a friend, showed the opposite pattern, a long-term positive effect.[8]

Selfless living results in greater overall life satisfaction.

---

## Selfless living results in greater overall life satisfaction.

---

Smith concluded, "A good life is a life of goodness—and that's something anyone can aspire to, no matter their dreams or circumstances."[9] This is a good reminder. Things that matter are not necessarily grand and remote goals. They can be simple things that are within the reach of us all. But they're still the best way to spend our days on this earth, causing us no regret when we come to look back on them.

Satirist P. J. O'Rourke said, "Everybody wants to save the earth; nobody wants to help Mom do the dishes."[10] Let's help Mom.

## The Joy of Helping

In our Things That Matter Survey, we asked, "Which generally gives you greater joy: fulfilling your own desires or helping other people?" I was very curious to see what the responses to this question would be.

How widespread is the perception that service beats selfishness in delivering happiness? I was thrilled to see that a clear majority—60 percent—answered "helping others." I bet you'd say that too.

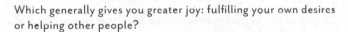

Which generally gives you greater joy: fulfilling your own desires or helping other people?

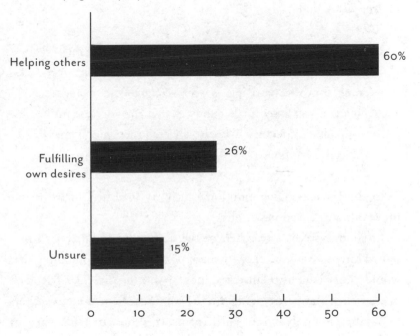

Empirical data backs up the intuitive sense many of us have that helping others has the power to help ourselves. Let me share just two more research results on this topic to further confirm your suspicion about the importance of living a selfless life.

Investigators at Columbia University were interested in finding out whether helping other people with their emotional well-being also benefited the helpers. So they conducted a study using an anonymous online platform. Participants shared stories about their own stressful life events. They could also provide emotional support to other participants by giving feedback, advice, and encouragement. And the outcome? "Participants who engaged more by helping others (vs. sharing and receiving support for their own problems) showed greater decreases in depression" and "by helping others . . . we may enhance our own regulatory skills and emotional well-being."[11]

An independent psychologist, commenting on this study for *Psychology Today*, said,

> The results showed that helping others to regulate their emotions predicted better emotional and cognitive outcomes for those participants who were *giving* the help. . . . Follow-up analyses further showed that this increase in reappraisal in people's lives also affected their mood and subjective happiness.[12]

In short, encouraging emotional recovery in others helps us improve our own emotional health.

In another study, researchers at the University of Pittsburgh presented forty-five volunteers with an opportunity to do something that would either benefit themselves, a charity, or a particular friend in need. When the participants' brains were scanned, the researchers found that "not only did the participants who chose to help a particular person display increased activity in two 'reward centers' of their brains, but they had *decreased* activity in three other areas that help inform the body's physical response to stress through blood pressure and inflammation." In other words, these people were both happier and calmer as a result of helping another individual.[13]

The evidence is clear that selfish pursuits don't bring the happiness we expect. Now we know what does.

We need to serve others if we're going to reach our full potential. And God knows the world needs us to serve.

## House of Misery

A few years ago, I was in the city of San Salvador, El Salvador, visiting the ten-by-twenty-foot home belonging to a woman named Lucilia. She was forty years old but could easily have passed for fifty, as the Salvadoran sun and the stresses of her life had prematurely aged her face. She lived in the house with her two daughters, ages fifteen and three. A few chickens occupied the yard, letting me know that Lucilia sold eggs, probably just a few each day, to support her family.

Tears streaking her weathered face, Lucilia shared with me the story of her fifteen-year-old daughter, Rachelle. For the previous two years, Rachelle had lived with a terminal disease that attacked her bones. It had left her body deformed and almost completely disabled. As a result of her disease, this beautiful teenager would soon lose her life. In the meantime, the disease was causing Rachelle pain that was both excruciating and unrelenting. Pain medications could help, and in fact there was a pharmacy right across the street that could have supplied them. But as Lucilia explained, the family simply did not have enough money to pay for the medications that could alleviate Rachelle's pain during the final phase of her life. A couple eggs sold each day doesn't provide for both food and medicine.

My heart broke for this girl and for her mother, who was in anguish because she couldn't help her daughter, whom she loved so much.

In the midst of this conversation, a different scene began to unfold on the floor of the dark and dirty home. While we were talking, Lucilia's three-year-old daughter, Anna, briefly left the room and then returned with one small bag of used crayons and one coloring book. Anna sat down on the tile floor, pulled two crayons from the bag, and opened her coloring book to the first page—it was already colored. So she flipped to the next page—it was also colored. As was the next . . . and the next . . . and the next . . . and the next . . . and the next—all colored. This was the only coloring book Anna had, and she'd used it all up. My heart again broke for this family. Oh, how I longed to run to my daughter's closet and grab just one of her many coloring books to give to this precious little girl!

The impact of poverty evidenced that morning was among the most powerful things I have ever witnessed. It made me wish all over again that those who have more than they need would share more with those who don't have enough.

Now, I am not naive enough to think that the cycle of poverty around the world will be broken simply by those of us who are advantaged choosing to hold on to less and give more. There are greater factors at play in the problem of poverty. But when you sit in the home of a dying fifteen-year-old girl whose mother can't afford the pain medication available across the street and the home of a little girl whose only coloring book is used up, you feel called to action. You begin to plead for the privilege of sharing with others. You realize that Lucilia's story is far too closely tied to yours. And it finally makes sense that there is nothing more fulfilling that you can pursue with your life than to help others.

I wish I could say that I was able to solve all of Lucilia's problems that day, but that's not always how the world works. But I did what I could. When we returned to the place we were staying in San Salvador, I took the little money left in my backpack and offered it to the leader of our trip. I asked him to see that Rachelle got some of that pain medication she needed. It wasn't much, but it was everything I had.

## And Then Comes Happiness

When we shift our focus off ourselves, we live lives of greater meaning and greater contribution. When we serve others without concern over what we might receive in return, we experience the beauty of selfless love. And when we direct our resources of time and money toward others, we begin to discover pursuits more valuable than material possessions, fame, beauty, or sex.

This is an important change in our worldview. Not just because the potential for contribution increases but also because our personal experience of happiness begins to grow.

Routinely asking the question "How does this action benefit someone else?" can serve as an important catalyst to change our views on almost everything we do. It immediately invites a new level of happiness into our lives.

Begin to serve a little. And then to serve some more. And then to make service a habit in your life. You'll find that you have fewer regrets about how you're living your life. And one day you'll realize that the bird of happiness is perched on your shoulder.

# 6

## Enough Is Enough
### Overcoming the Distraction of Money

Money won't make you happy . . . but everybody wants
to find out for themselves.

—Zig Ziglar

One Friday evening, when I was in my early thirties, I found myself
in the passenger seat of a friend's vehicle. We had just gone out for
dinner, as we did once a month. He was further along in his career
path than I was and graciously gave up time each month to invest in
and mentor me. As was always the case, he paid for dinner, never even
giving me the chance to request the check, and left a generous tip.

On this particular ride, as we pulled into my neighborhood, I asked
a question that popped into my head: "Were you always this generous, or was there a specific moment when you decided to become
generous?" I don't know if he could tell or not, but I had a personal
motivation for asking the question. I was starting to question the use
of my money and wanted to become more generous with it.

At first, he tried to dodge the question by claiming he wasn't par-
ticularly generous and never thought of himself in that way. But I
persisted. I had learned much about generosity from him, specifically
that financial generosity comes in a number of forms and you don't
need to be wealthy to have your life defined by it.

When I finally got him to answer the question—we were sitting in my driveway by this time—he filled my spirit with hope. "No, Joshua, I wasn't always a generous person," he said. "But at some point in my life, it occurred to me that all the men and women I looked up to and wanted to emulate were generous people. And I decided that day I would work harder at it."

My friend's observation was true then—and still is today. When we consider the men and women we most want to emulate with our lives, aren't they also the most generous among us? They are kind, loving, thoughtful, and selfless. They are quick to share their time, money, talents, and spirit. There may be times when we wish to be rich, but deep down we realize that the people we most admire are generous, not wealthy. And at some point in our lives, if we are to reach the end with little regret, we must make the decision to be so as well.

> When we consider the men and women we most want to emulate with our lives, aren't they also the most generous among us?

But why is this so difficult? Is it because our desire for money is more persistent than we realize?

## Cash Craving

A well-known proverb goes like this: "The love of money is the root of all kinds of evil."[1] And I haven't met many people who would disagree.

But here's the thing with that saying—nobody thinks they *love* money. When we hear a phrase like "the love of money is the root of all kinds of evil," most of us assume that *someone else* needs to hear that message—our bosses, our spouses, our friends down the street, or that corporate billionaire recently in the news. We don't often see ourselves in the old proverb.

Nobody *loves* money . . . but everybody sure wants more of it.

Is there ever a time when enough is enough?

Money is the biggest source of stress among Americans, with around 70 percent of income earners worrying about money regularly.[2] This despite the fact that the United States is one of the wealthiest nations in the history of the world. How can that be the case? Why would 70 percent of people in such a wealthy nation be stressed out about money? Is it because we don't have enough? Are 70 percent of us lacking food or shelter or clothing? No, that's not it.

If you think you can outearn your desire for money, you are mistaken. Even those most of us would consider rich don't think they have enough money. For example, 87 percent of millionaires would not say they are wealthy.[3] In one Boston College study, people with an average net worth of $78 million felt they needed 25 percent more wealth to be content.[4] Even John D. Rockefeller, the richest man in American history, when asked by a reporter, "How much money is enough?" is said to have answered, "Just a little bit more."

In most cases, we don't feel stressed about money because we don't have enough; we feel stressed about money because we simply want more of it.

---

We don't feel stressed about money because we don't have enough; we feel stressed about money because we simply want more of it.

---

We look to money to provide things it is unable to provide (namely, happiness and security). We think, *If I just made X or had Y saved, I'd feel secure and happy.* But then we reach that number and don't feel happy or secure. Rather than thinking, *Maybe I was looking for happiness in the wrong place,* we just change the number. *Oh, actually, if I had Z, I'd feel happy and secure.* But it never happens . . . because money *never* provides lasting happiness or security, even though we're constantly stressed out by thinking that it should.

In the Things That Matter Survey, we asked, "How likely are you to be happier in life if you had more money?" Would you believe that 79 percent of the respondents said they would be happier if they had more money? Of course you would believe that. Because most of us think the same thing!

How likely are you to be happier in life if you had more money?

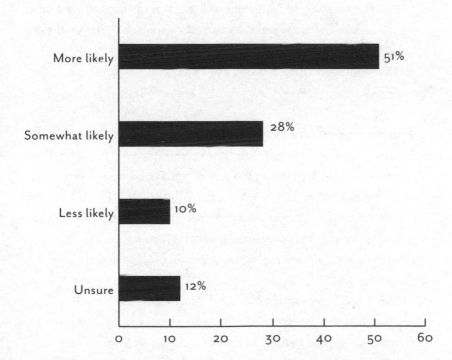

We also asked a follow-up question: "How often does your desire for acquiring more money influence your daily decisions?" Almost 70 percent of respondents said their desire for acquiring more money influences their daily decisions sometimes, frequently, or always.

Does your desire for acquiring more money influence your daily decisions?

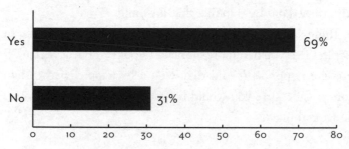

How are we going to live generous lives focused on things that matter if our daily decisions are so focused on acquiring more money because we think it will make us happier? We can't.

The sooner we figure that out, the better.

## The Reformed Lawyer

Several years ago, Jay Harrington was an ambitious, hardworking lawyer in metro Detroit. In addition to that job, he and his wife, Heather, owned Harrington, a brand-strategy and design agency that specialized in providing creative solutions for professional-services firms. By all appearances, Jay was highly successful in both of his jobs, making a lot of money.

But inside he was miserable.

"The days dragged by while the years seemed to fly past," Jay remembered. "I spent more time living through a screen than appreciating the wonders of the real world."[5] *What is wrong with me?* he asked himself. Eventually he realized he'd lost his zest for living. He was *funding* a life but not *living* a life.

One thing he considered important was being connected to nature and the rhythms of the days going by. Another was having enough time for Heather and their three girls. He didn't know exactly what achieving all this would look like, but he knew he had to take steps to move in that direction. Here's the story of what happened, in his own words:

> I took a deep breath and got to work.
>
> I left the law firm I founded. . . .
>
> We sold our house. We moved from an expensive sub-urb to a small town in northern Michigan with our three young girls. We took steps back in order to create space and time so that we could make a clear-eyed decision about the path we would follow once we were ready to move forward again. . . .
>
> Like Thoreau, we "went to the woods" to live more de-liberately.
>
> Fast forward five years later, and I am busier than ever between the responsibilities of work and family. And also happier than ever.
>
> The big difference is that I'm busy on my own terms, in a place of my choosing. My ambition is undiminished—but it's not consuming me. I'm focused on what matters to me, not all the trappings of "success" that merely get in the way of a meaningful life.[6]

Today, Jay calls himself a "reformed lawyer." With his wife, he still runs their design agency. They don't make as much money as they used to, but it's enough. Neither one of them regrets their choices, because now they're living in a way that makes more room for family, fun, and the joys of nature.

## Limiting Our Potential

Money choices force us to look into our hearts. Specifically, we need to consider if we've made money an end in itself, rather than a means to provide or do what we consider important. Those who live their lives constantly desiring money fall into a trap—a trap that leaves us with empty promises, unfulfilled desires, and handicapped potential.

> We need to consider if we've made money an end in itself, rather than a means to provide or do what we consider important.

One reason is that the desire for money can never be satisfied. It is a hopeless love that always desires more. And more than that, it keeps us, our attitudes, and our actions in bondage. When the love of money is present, fulfillment is not, because we are constantly held hostage by the pursuit of material wealth.

The pursuit of money begins to consume our time, energy, and focus. Whether we're thinking about how to find it, make it, grow it, or save it, the desire to acquire more results in our constantly directing our attention toward it. There is opportunity to increase wealth all around us, all the time. Whether it's working overtime, chasing a new client, starting a side hustle, or managing our investments, the pursuit of money requires our time and energy.

But that's not all. The pursuit of money begins to circumvent and even alter our values. When the desire for money is present in our lives, we become almost different people, often engaging in behaviors we would otherwise avoid. The desire fuels competition against others. The love of money requires me to desire what you already possess. For me to gain more, you must part with yours. The world quickly becomes a zero-sum game dominated by jealousy and envy.

The desire for money begins to dominate our time, our energy, our values, and our relationships. Too often, it limits our potential to bring good into the world, because we can never become greater than that which we most desire. When the acquisition of money becomes our greatest goal in life, we can never become greater than the balance in our bank account. And that's a shame, because we have so many better things to offer this world.

Now, it's important to note that money isn't evil in and of itself. Money is amoral or neutral in itself—technically, it's just a means to facilitate the exchange of goods and services. If our heart is in the wrong place, it can lead to "all kinds of evil." If we're generous hearted, money can be used for all kinds of good. But that is different from living a life of constantly pursuing money.

I should also point out that the act of making money isn't evil. Everyone should be adequately compensated for the work that they do, and some people are especially gifted at it—give them a nickel, and they can't help but turn it into a quarter. I'm not speaking against wages, compensation, or profit. Please don't mistake this to be a chapter on not working hard. (I'm going to talk specifically about that in chapter 9.) Working hard is different from desiring wealth.

So this isn't about how much money we have. The bigger question that we need to answer here is this: Are we wasting too much of our one life—desiring money and always striving to get more of it? Because when we do, we will inevitably be distracted from things that matter in the long run. When is enough enough?

## Maybe We Don't Need More Money

I try to remember that everyone is unique, with a unique background and focused on unique passions. We are different in our nationalities, heritages, genders, family statuses, religions, cultures, and worldviews. But I am becoming increasingly convinced there is one characteristic that unites each of us: we think we need more money than we actually do.

### We think we need more money than we actually do.

Of course, there are many in the world who do need more money for legitimate survival. But that does not include me. And it probably does not include you. Most likely, you already make enough to provide for your needs—probably more than enough. After all, if you're reading this book, you are an educated person who has access to books and the leisure and liberty to reflect on your life goals. You probably live in one of the more developed nations of the world. You're not struggling to achieve the first rung on Maslow's hierarchy of needs. But our circumstance is rarer than you might think.

The World Bank said that in 2017 . . .

- 9.2 percent of the world's population lived on less than $1.90 a day,
- 24.1 percent of the world lived on less than $3.20 a day, and
- 43.6 percent on less than $5.50 a day.[7]

Just stop and think how *you* would get by on $5.50 a day. Is it even imaginable? In America today, there is an argument that the current minimum *hourly* wage ought to be $15—three times the amount that 44 percent of the world's population makes in an entire day! To carry this even further and put your financial circumstance into perspective, if your family of four makes $50,000 a year, you're in the top 10.6 percent of people on the planet for income.[8]

Poverty is still incredibly prevalent in our world, and we need to alleviate that. In fact, I hope more of us will take up the challenge to confront and end it.

But let's discuss something that isn't usually talked about. There are consequences and temptations that accompany poverty, and we can all guess what they are. But wealth brings consequences and temptations of its own.

People with money tend to be more isolated and lonelier than others, as I pointed out in the previous chapter. They can emphasize individualism and self-reliance at the expense of community, and they can exhibit a lack of empathy, a sense of entitlement, and arrogance.[9] Did you know that the more expensive the car a driver has, the more likely he or she is to commit driving infractions, such as failing to stop for a pedestrian in a crosswalk?[10]

It is true that having more money isn't the secret to having more happiness. It doesn't solve all our problems. In many cases, it brings new ones. As Benjamin Franklin said, "Money never made a man happy yet, nor will it. The more a man has, the more he wants. Instead of its filling a vacuum, it makes one."[11] Perhaps the greatest danger of wealth is that nobody appreciates when they achieve it . . . they continually desire more. That's why people in the top 10 percent of the world can still think they don't have enough.

I once interviewed a man named Daniel Suelo who had decided to live without money—*completely* without money. I was sitting in an airport in Charlotte when I first came across his story and immediately reached out via email to see if we could talk. I had to hear more. He graciously agreed.

For years now, Daniel has lived in a variety of outdoor locations, including a cave in Utah. He gets his food by fishing and foraging for berries and other edibles. He walks into a nearby town and gets food out of dumpsters.

Why is he doing this? Partly because he wants to prove that it's possible to live outside the economic grid. Partly because he wants to have minimal ecological impact. Regardless of the *why,* Daniel proves that one can live a meaningful life on zero dollars. The most profound thing I heard him say was "Money only exists if two or more people believe it exists."

I think we get into the mindset that money is such a valuable resource and can bring all sorts of good into our lives, so much so that we literally plan our days around how to get more of it. But when you get down to it, it's just pieces of paper and rounded pieces of metal (or numbers stored in a computer). It has value only because we believe it does . . . or because the government says so.

Sure, money expedites trade. But is there a chance we've exalted its value too much in our affections? I'm sure of it. And it's to our own detriment.

Suelo is an extreme example, and you probably don't want to live in a cave any more than I do. But his story goes to show that even in modern developed nations, it's possible to live with less money, or even none. And once we begin to see that, a whole new freedom of opportunity begins to emerge in our lives.

A few years ago, *USA Today* published an article titled "Price Tag for the American Dream: $130K a Year." To arrive at his price tag, the author added up all the expenses it took for a family of four to lead healthy and personally fulfilling lives. Among their expenses: $17,000 a year for a mortgage, over $12,500 a year for groceries, $11,000 a year for a vehicle, and more for vacations, insurance, education, and retirement savings. Based on his calculations, the author said, "It's clear . . . fewer and fewer of us can afford to live it."[12]

I read the article when it was first published and knew immediately it was hogwash. Despite having a family of four that had lived quite contently and comfortably in four different states, I had never made half that amount per year. I knew firsthand the American Dream doesn't cost $130,000 a year.

But I feared the responses of others who would read the article. When the world around us constantly screams that we need more money to live the good life, we quickly fall into the temptation of thinking that we don't have enough, rather than realizing that most of us already are wealthy.

I've lived as a minimalist for the last twelve years, and one of the most life-giving benefits I've realized along the way is that we need so much less than we think we need. Many of the minimalists I've met have proved that they can live a good life on far less than they originally thought. Most people don't have an earning problem; they have a spending problem.

We don't really *need* more money. We just want it.

We'd like more cash in our pockets. We want bigger paychecks. We want a larger balance in our checking accounts, savings accounts, or retirement accounts. And many of us have tied our happiness to this pursuit of money.

Even though our basic needs have been met, our desire for money persists. Far too often, this desire begins to take root as a perceived *need* inside us. Before we know it, we forget that we're talking about a *want* and begin confusing it with a *need*. And the financial stress of never having enough begins to emerge. But, in reality, what we *need* and what we *want* are rarely the same.

## If we spent less time trying to get more money, we would have more time and energy and margin for other things.

And if we spent less time trying to get more money, we would have more time and energy and margin for other things. If we needed less money for ourselves, we would have more money to spend on the pursuits that are most meaningful to us.

## Saving for What?

Greg McBride, the chief financial analyst for Bankrate.com, once said, "Nothing lets you sleep better at night than knowing you have money tucked away to cover unplanned expenses."[13] And I agree, at least to some extent. There is wisdom in saving money for future seasons of unplanned need.

But is it possible to save too much?

I can tell you one thing—that's not the subject of an article you're going to find in any of the popular money magazines. And I can't remember ever seeing a financial advisory firm's commercial on television warning that we may be keeping too much for ourselves. This is a countercultural question. But is it possible to lead a life of greater significance and impact when we do wrestle with it?

Consider this viewpoint. When we save, we set aside money for potential future needs. But this saving always comes with an opportunity cost. By its nature, saving for *potential, personal* needs in the *future* comes at the expense of meeting *somebody's real* need *today*.

Everywhere we look, we see needs all around us. Approximately

820 million people do not have enough food to eat, 768 million live without access to an improved source of water, and 2.5 billion people in our world today live without proper sanitation.[14] Men and women in your hometown live in cardboard boxes or under the bridge. Orphans need homes. Single mothers need financial assistance. Battered women need a fresh start. The disadvantaged need level playing fields. Your neighbor down the street needs help with his medical bills. There are countless people living today with deep and painful emotional, spiritual, and physical needs.

And our money can work to fix these problems right now. Our dollars can solve problems of health and injustice and inequality.

But rather than help to feed the homeless family down the street, we choose to set aside a portion of our money *just in case* we ever find ourselves in the same situation. Rather than properly funding elementary education in the heart of our cities, we set aside tens of thousands of dollars for our sons and daughters to attend premier colleges. Rather than donating money to buy soup for the hungry today, we hope to save enough to serve prime rib at our daughter's wedding reception. Rather than helping to create affordable housing for the homeless, the average American is striving to save $1.7 million for his or her retirement.[15]

Does this really sound like the best possible use of our money?

Or are we so concerned with our own comfort and security that we can't even recognize the opportunity to do something greater with our lives? Isn't this just another way that wanting more money gets in the way of things that actually matter?

You've probably heard about the abysmal savings rates in the United States and other countries. And it's true: too few people save money. Nearly three-quarters of all US employees are living paycheck to paycheck, while almost three in ten adults have no emergency savings at all.[16] And if that's you, it would be a good idea to get a handle on

where your money is going and cut down your expenses wherever possible, because it's still wise to save money for the future. And maybe
that is the message you need to take from this chapter.

But for those of us who are overspending on ourselves or oversav-
ing for potential needs that may or may not ever arise, choose to err
on the side of generosity. In the end, you'll be prouder of the money
you gave to others than the money you kept for yourself.

---

## You'll be prouder of the money you gave to others than the money you kept for yourself.

---

You can begin avoiding regret today if you'll . . .

## Start giving a little more.

## Try This

---

If you're stressed about money (which is apparently 70 percent of us),
the quickest way to alleviate that stress and change your outlook is to
give some money away—literally the opposite of what you've been
trying in the past. Which is good, because clearly whatever we've been
doing to try to alleviate financial stress isn't working.

Try this as an experiment: give away five dollars this week. You can
drop it in an offering plate, put it in a red kettle outside Walmart, or
donate via any number of charities' websites. At the end of the week,
see if you still have food, a roof, and clothing. You will. Your needs
will still be met. Test it out again next week. After a few weeks of your
needs being met, try giving ten dollars a week. Again, you will dis-

cover that there is food on your table and a roof over your head. The goal here is not to give away just a few dollars per week; the goal is to notice how your needs are being met *and* how you had extra to spare.

(I know you may already be giving to charity. If so, add five or ten or even fifty dollars to your next week's donation. And notice if your needs are still being met. They will be.)

In that moment, you will discover the greatest benefit of generosity. It changes our understanding of enough. It shows us how much we have to give and how much good we can accomplish. It helps us see the needs of those we live alongside and begins to alleviate them.

That is a lesson my mom learned from her mother. My grandmother had a reputation for being incredibly generous, so it was not uncommon for someone to knock on the Salems' front door asking for money. My mom told me that more than once, when she was a child, she saw a stranger come to the door and tell Grandma a story about financial hardship. My grandma would, almost without fail, give money to the person.

From her upstairs room, my mom would peek out the window and watch the transaction take place. As a young girl, she couldn't make sense of the situation. Why would her mom give money to a stranger, especially when they were so poor themselves? But as she got older, she began to understand. "My parents were generous people who wanted to help when they saw a need. And you know what? We never had much, but we always had enough. And looking back, those memories of watching my mother help people in need brings me far more joy today than anything else we could have purchased."

Sometimes generosity benefits the giver as much as the receiver.

## Today Versus Tomorrow

When I got my first book-advance payment, our regular expenses were already being covered from my other work. So, in a sense, the advance money was extra. As minimalists, my wife and I were not about to go out and buy a bunch of stuff with it. But then what *were* we going to do with it? We came up with a plan.

At that time, I had a conversation with my sister, Jana, about the book advance. We were in the backyard of my home, enjoying a beautiful Phoenix fall evening.

"What are you going to do with the money?" she asked.

"We're going to use it to create a nonprofit organization that changes how the world cares for orphans by focusing on family-based solutions in developing nations."

After a brief moment of silence, Jana responded by saying, "Oh. I guess I thought you would put the money away for your kids' college fund or something."

Recalling our shared personal history, I reminded her, "But our parents didn't set aside any money for us to go to college. We both went, and so did our brother. And everything has turned out just fine for all of us."

"Yeah," she replied, "but things are different now. College is much more expensive than when we went to school."

She had a point: the costs of college tuition have risen drastically in the past two or three decades. Briefly, I thought perhaps I *should* put the money away to fund our two kids' education. But no, my decision had already been cemented by an important truth concerning lasting security.

My response went something like this: "Jana, do you really think that if I use this money to help orphans find families, there won't be any money available for my kids to go to college when the time comes?

I just refuse to believe that is how the world works. In my experience, I have seen generosity returned to the giver over and over again."

"Well," she said, "when you say it that way, it does seem to make sense."

We are wise to plan for the future and provide for our families. But as we do, we should consider our desire for financial advancement against the backdrop of things that matter and others' real needs today. Maybe it's more important to be generous right now and trust that our future needs will be met when the time comes. As a bonus for our generosity, we'll find that giving generously offers a reward of joy.

## A Warm Glow

Stop and think about a time when giving away money made you feel good inside. It wasn't a unique experience, and you're far from alone.

Extensive international research suggests that prosocial spending (using your financial resources to help others) provides emotional benefits to the givers across the board—it's considered a likely "psychological universal." For example, in one study, "participants in Canada and South Africa [who were] randomly assigned to buy items for charity reported higher levels of positive affect than participants who were assigned to buy the same items for themselves." The findings suggest that once we overcome whatever resistance we may have to being generous, "the reward experienced from helping others" is something we can count on, regardless of our cultural or economic context.[17]

A different study by some of the same authors concluded, "Both correlational and experimental studies have shown that people who spend money on others report more happiness. The benefits of such *prosocial spending* emerge among adults around the world, and the warm glow of giving can be detected even in toddlers."[18]

## What a Free Puppy Is Worth

My friend Kevin has three daughters, the youngest of whom is named Sophia. She has always been the saver of the family, squirreling away every bit of allowance or cash gift she receives. At the age of nine, she had two hundred dollars in her piggy bank.

Sophia had also, for the longest time, wanted a puppy. And when she noticed a handmade flyer at the local coffee shop from a farmer giving away free puppies, she jumped at the chance and quickly convinced her dad to drive out to the farm the next day.

Upon arrival, it didn't take long to notice the small farmhouse and humble, frugal lifestyle of the struggling farmer and his wife. They worked hard with their hands every day, but their small family-owned farm was barely staying afloat.

After visiting with the farmer and playing with the puppies, Kevin and Sophia promised to make a decision by the morning. My friend Kevin had already resigned himself to the fact they were getting a puppy, but first he had an important life lesson to teach Sophia.

"I wanted to teach my daughter about responsibility, hard work, and discipline," Kevin told me. "So that evening I asked her if she was willing to pay for the dog with her own money."

"But the puppies are free," she replied.

"Yes, I know," Kevin said. "But think about all the love and care that farmer and his wife have invested into our puppy's life. And they clearly don't have much. Don't you think it would be nice to give them something even though the puppies are free?"

It was true that Kevin thought it would be nice for them to help the farm couple. But he also thought that if Sophia spent some of her money for the puppy, it would help her take her responsibility to the puppy more seriously.

"I'd like you to go up to your room and think about how much you'd like to offer the farmer as a gift. Then come tell me. It's entirely up to you."

Soberly, Sophia went upstairs to her room.

About five minutes later, she came bounding down the steps.

"I would like to give him one hundred dollars for the puppy," she said with a smile.

Kevin was caught off guard by the generous offer, almost spilling his drink when he heard it. He had thought twenty-five dollars would be a nice gesture. He never dreamed his perpetual-saver daughter would give up half of her savings for the puppy.

Not sure how to respond, Kevin thought that maybe, if she thought about it a bit longer, she'd change her mind and lower her offer. After all, the puppies had been offered for free.

So he responded, "Wow, that sure is a big number. Maybe you should think some more about if you really want to give that much. Why don't you go back up to your room and really think through this decision? Take longer than five minutes this time. And then whatever you decide will be our final decision."

She walked back up the stairs.

Fifteen minutes later, Kevin was starting to wonder if Sophia had been distracted by something else and forgotten the assignment. But just as he was getting ready to retrieve her, her head popped around the corner as she neared the stairs. The skip had returned to her step.

Kevin looked forward to hearing the new decision. The longer he had thought about his daughter giving up half her saved money for the *free* puppy, the more he looked forward to her returning with a lower number. This dog would cost them plenty of money in the future anyway.

"Well, what did you decide?" he asked.

I hope you will not forget her answer. I certainly haven't.

"Well," she began, "I was thinking about what you said about how much work they've put in already, providing a nice home for the puppy. And then I started looking around my room and thinking about this nice house that we live in and all the nice stuff we have and how the farmer and his wife have so little. And so, Dad, I've decided to change how much money I would like to give them for the puppy. Rather than one hundred dollars, I would like to give them all two hundred dollars in my piggy bank."

## Humble Greatness

Stories of generosity move us and inspire us. Celebrities may get the headlines, but it is the real-world examples of sacrificial giving—such as Sophia emptying her piggy bank—that motivate us to do the same.

A column about the adoptive mother in Minneapolis who dedicates two evenings a month to a nonprofit placing orphans in loving homes doesn't sell many newspapers. The struggling mechanic in Nashville who is a father of three and makes a five-hundred-dollar donation to a cause he believes in doesn't trend on Twitter. The middle-class family who gives away 10 percent of their income to their church every week doesn't drive much internet traffic. The widow who lives in a humble home but continues to give will rarely appear on the evening news. But these are real people changing lives and making a difference. You can be one of them.

When my parents were young and poor, struggling to raise three kids under the age of two, an anonymous person once left a fifty-dollar bill in an envelope in their mailbox. That unexpected money allowed my parents to buy groceries for the week. That story of generosity was told countless times at our dinner table growing up, and it's still repeated at family gatherings today (and now in this book). One simple gesture of generosity, many years ago, has now touched countless lives. Just like the simple act of a mentor paying for my dinner on that quiet evening in Vermont.

That is how generosity affects us. It moves us to become better people and inspires others to do the same. But when we live our lives constantly pursuing riches, generosity will always elude us. You cannot both be generous and chase wealth.

The more we remove ourselves from the empty pursuit of money, the more we are drawn to others-centered living. And the more we are drawn to helping others, the greater lives of lasting significance we end up living.

# 7

---

## Litter on the Road to Purpose
### *Overcoming the Distraction of Possessions*

Simplicity . . . brings sanity to our compulsive extrava-
gance, and peace to our frantic spirit. . . . . It allows us to
see material things for what they are—goods to enhance
life, not to oppress life. People once again become more
important than possessions.

—RICHARD FOSTER, *FREEDOM OF SIMPLICITY*

In 2017, I was invited to speak to a large men's conference in Warsaw,
Poland, about minimalism. I knew that Poland had regained its independence only three decades earlier, but I was reminded of that reality
at the opening banquet when my translator, a man my age, spoke
about staring at bread lines outside his apartment window throughout
his teenage years. It became clearer to me how different our backgrounds were.

Transition from Soviet-imposed communism to free-market ways
had been rough, and the Polish economy was still relatively small.
Most Poles were not as wealthy as people in the West, meaning that,
compared to some other nations, Poland was not as plagued with con-
spicuous consumption. Nevertheless, its personal disposable income
was on the rise, so materialism could easily become more of a problem
for this nation.

My message for those in attendance that day? Take every advantage of your freedoms and entrepreneurial opportunities. In so doing, however, do not lose sight of the things that matter most. And keep your freedoms centered on pursuits that will be important in the long run. In other words, it was the message of *Things That Matter*.

Following my presentation, I sat down with Darek Cupiał, the organizer of the event, over dinner (pierogies, of course). Darek said, "Joshua, can I tell you more about why I invited you here today?"

From across the table, I could tell he was debating whether or not to share with me what he was thinking. "Of course," I said. "Please do."

He began to tell me a story. "When I was younger, I had an important mentor. He was a survivor of Auschwitz who would live almost his entire existence in an occupied Poland—occupied first by the Germans and then by the Communist Party of the Soviet Union.

"This man once made an observation to me I have never forgotten. After a trip he had taken to Western Europe, he pulled me aside and said, 'I have come to realize that materialism holds people captive in many of the same ways communism does. The communism I grew up with sought to destroy our personal identities by force. Materialism does the same. But materialism destroys personal identity by choice.'

"And that is why I wanted you here today, Joshua. To inspire us, both as individuals and as a society, to not use our newfound freedom to acquire further bondage."

I wish I'd known that wise old Auschwitz survivor. He seems to have been able to see deeper into reality than most of us. At any rate, he was right about the destruction that our property and possessions can cause to our souls. We're so steeped in materialism, and take it so much for granted, that we may have trouble even seeing the problem. Even worse, we live in a society that champions the pursuit and accumulation of material possessions—"the more, the better" is the mantra we are raised to believe. Yet one of our greatest distractions from pursuing our goals is our hoard of material goods.

Who can go gung ho after a challenging goal if they're constantly buying and taking care of a bunch of stuff? Who can invest in things that matter when they're too busy organizing the garage? We're drowning in possessions, and all too often our dreams are drowning with us.

I've been speaking and writing about minimalism for a decade and a half now. After all that time, I've come to believe that the number one benefit of minimalism is this: it frees up your money, time, and energy to pursue your greatest passions. In fact, I would say that changing your attitude toward material ownership and getting control of your possessions is a *necessary step* to fulfilling your potential. And it's doable for everyone.

Every time someone tells me, "I could never be a minimalist," I think to myself, *But you already are.* Because everybody is minimizing something. If you're not minimizing your possessions, you're minimizing your money, time, and potential.

---

## If you're not minimizing your possessions, you're minimizing your money, time, and potential.

---

So look around at your stuff. Some of these things may in effect be *trophies* of your success. Some of them may be *toys* you thought would make your life happier. But if they're not *tools* to help you accomplish your goals in life, maybe the time is already here for you to start getting rid of a lot of them. On second thought, strike that "maybe."

## Immortality Projects

In chapter 3, I mentioned the anthropologist Ernest Becker, who said, "What man really fears is not so much extinction, but extinction *with insignificance.*" Becker went on to say that "in order for anything once alive to have meaning, its effects must remain alive in eternity in some way." Attempting to defeat death, outlive our mortality, and overcome our terror of dying, we secure what Becker called "immortality symbols" for ourselves.[1]

These symbols can take many forms, but Becker wrote that most modern people in capitalist societies turn to wealth and possessions as their immortality projects. "Money gives power *now*—and, through accumulated property, land, and interest, power in the future." He contended that the pursuit of wealth and possessions is so common, it's "no wonder economic equality is beyond the endurance of modern democratic man: the house, the car, the bank balance are his immortality symbols."[2]

Few people desire a world with such economic inequality as now exists, but that is what happens when our desires are misplaced. When the pursuit of possessions and property takes center stage in our lives, not only do we sell short our potential, but we also experience negative effects, both personal and societal. Some accumulate little and wish they had more. Some accumulate much and feel prideful . . . yet also strangely dissatisfied.

We pursue possessions and property in an often subconscious desire to outlive ourselves. But we end up regretting it in the end. You know why? Because there are better ways to outlive ourselves! There is an inheritance that we can leave and instill in others that's greater than the size of our homes or the designer names on our clothing. Nobody is going to stand up at your funeral and say, "He had a really expensive couch" or "She owned a lot of nice shoes." Much more importantly, our legacies include the examples we live, the moral compasses we set, the characters we develop, and the names we build for ourselves and our families.

---

## Our legacies include the examples we live, the moral compasses we set, the characters we develop, and the names we build for ourselves and our families.

---

If you stop to think about it, you already know your possessions are not the best immortality symbols to be chasing. You want to be remembered for being loving, giving, and present. You want your life to have mattered for something important. And believe it or not, the pursuit and accumulation of material possessions often runs contrary to that pursuit, as they naturally require your time, money, and focus.

One example of somebody who began to pursue bigger dreams for her life than material possessions is Elaine, who is doing something inventive and generous with her home.

## A New Dream for the Dream Home

At the age of sixty, Elaine was living in a beautiful house on an acreage outside Birmingham, Alabama. She shared the home with her twenty-nine-year-old daughter, Rebecca, who had severe special needs. Elaine's husband had left years earlier. Now her other children were grown and had moved out too.

Elaine recalled of that time, "I was living in a beautiful home. My husband and I built it ourselves. But now it was only a museum to the past. It was filled with the possessions of my deceased parents, the possessions of a failed marriage, and the possessions of three grown children now gone. There were entire closets I dreaded opening the door to."

Rebecca needed almost constant care, and it had come down to Elaine to give this care. She knew she had to simplify her life in order to stretch her ability to take care of Rebecca's needs. And so she began removing the possessions from her life that were no longer useful. "I just wanted to be able to quickly put my hands on whatever I needed in that moment to care for my daughter," she said.

But her dreams quickly became bigger than mere organization. "As I aged, I began to wonder how I could continue to care for Rebecca. Decluttering and beginning to see how owning less was perfecting me. I began to see a road forward. I also began to see the special needs of other kids, young adults, and their parents in my community. As I cleared out the clutter, I began hosting events at my home—not just for special needs children but also for their parents, who so desperately need respite."

She brought in some animals to live on the acreage and created spaces in her home for art and music in a way that would be engaging for people with special needs. She found volunteers and workers to staff these parties and events and has even helped to bring about changes in how the community cares for adults with special needs.

Today, her home is being modified to accommodate the needs of young-adult women with special needs. Eventually, she hopes for it to become the home for four young adults (one of them Rebecca), staffed with caregivers and equipped with creative spaces for art, music, nature, and animals.

Elaine has made a different provision for herself. "I am planning to build a small cottage on the back of the property that will eventually be my home so I can remain close to my daughter. A large home filled with stuff is no longer what I dream of most. I am pursuing something greater with my life now."

## Three Ways Our Possessions Distract Us from Things That Matter

Possessions, while necessary up to a point, begin after that point to become an impediment to and a distraction from living a meaningful life. Having too many possessions slows us down in the pursuit of what we care about. In the worst cases, it may prevent us from making any progress at all. How sad to think that those clothes we bought from the clearance rack or that furniture we ordered from IKEA or that stuff we splurged on from Amazon during the COVID-19 pandemic would stop us from fulfilling our highest potential.

As you read about these three ways property and possessions can be a distraction, ask yourself which one is the biggest problem for you.

### 1. Tying Up Our Money

*Oniomania* is the technical name for shopping addiction, or compulsive buying disorder. It's been around a long time, but its prevalence has been fueled in recent years by online shopping. Like other addictions, it is a way of self-treating negative emotions and low self-esteem. Few of us would admit to having a shopping addiction, or at least one that fits a clinical definition. But I can't help wondering, as I look at our overfilled closets, drawers too stuffed to close, and garages used so heavily for storage that we can't park in them, if we're all suffering from compulsive buying more than we think.

Jessica Pishko was happy living in New York and working at a corporate law firm. But life began going downhill for her when she started filling up her little apartment with things she'd bought in the stores of Manhattan. When her closets got full, she stuffed new clothes (with the price tags still on) under her bed.

In her memoir, *In the Red*, she wrote about buying a $2,200 fur coat she didn't have the money for. It reveals the sad compulsions of the shopping addict.

> The salesperson pulled the jacket off the model and put it
> on me. It was like being wrapped in a warm hug—the
> shearling was incredibly soft. The color was rich and
> slightly dangerous. Looking in the mirror, I felt worthy
> and valued. . . .
> I took the coat off and stroked it as I would a lover.[3]

Pishko arranged a layaway plan with installment payments. "I continually brought my $200 to the store, my most constant commitment," she said. "At the time, I began sending my rent a week late, sometimes more. I paid my parents most weeks. But I always gave the saleswoman my $200." Finally she paid her final installment. "Back in my apartment, I opened the bag and buried my face in the soft fur."[4]

How sad that dead animal fur, priced higher than she could really afford, was what Pishko valued most at that time. Thankfully, she began to see how distorted her priorities had become. Yet it would take her two lost jobs, $30,000 in debt, and bankruptcy before she could face her demons. She "finally learned that the bumpy road to recovery is easier to travel without all the shopping bags."

Most of us can look at Jessica Pishko's story and think, *Wow, she had real problems.* But how many of us do the same thing, just not as extreme? We get emotionally attached to possessions. We buy things we don't need. We buy even if it drives us deeper into debt.

Or we read her story and wonder, *Who in their right mind would buy a fur coat rather than pay their rent?* Let me rephrase that. *Who in their right mind would buy something they don't need when their money could be used for something more important?* Suddenly, Jessica's story looks a bit more like ours.

Are we more focused on helping others, or are we more focused on consuming for ourselves?

It's interesting to note that in the United States, charitable giving as a percentage of the GDP has remained constant at around 2 percent for decades.[5] Meanwhile, the US GDP has grown from $543 billion in 1960 to over $21 trillion in 2019.[6] We're getting richer, but we're not getting more generous. Where's all the extra money going? We're spending it on ourselves. In fact, the average American now spends $18,000 a year on nonessentials.[7]

For myself, I want to devote my money to the causes I care about with all the commitment and anticipation that Jessica Pishko had when she delivered her two-hundred-dollar layaway payments for a fur coat she didn't need. That's how you live a life you're proud of in the end.

But the money we spend is just one aspect of how possessions can distract us from things that matter.

## 2. Using Up Our Time

John Ruskin, an art critic in the nineteenth century, once wrote, "Every increased possession loads us with a new weariness."[8] Two centuries later, the statement is truer than ever. Every single thing you own requires a little bit of your attention and time, whether it be researching, shopping, cleaning, organizing, repairing, replacing, recycling, or working just to make the money to buy the new thing that you can take home to clean and organize and replace.

# Every single thing you own requires a little bit of your attention and time.

According to the American Time Use Survey, the average American spends almost two hours a day taking care of his or her house, including maintenance, repair, decoration, gardening, laundry, internal cleaning, and kitchen duties. Men spend one hour and twenty-five minutes a day on household activities, while women spend two hours and fifteen minutes on such activities.[9] I don't know about you, but I'd like some of that time back for more interesting endeavors.

If you think time-saving devices (robotic vacuums, smart slow cookers, and so on) are on their way to saving us from spending so much time on our homes, don't count on it. Combined hours devoted to home care have remained relatively constant since 1900.[10] Some of our devices probably do save us time, but our increased number of possessions offsets the gains.

Look around at your own home. All that clutter used to be money and time. The more you own, the greater the burden on your life your possessions become. And most people have no idea how big a burden their possessions have become until they begin to remove them.

If you want to live a more meaningful life focused on the things that matter, own less stuff. But more on that in a moment. Because there is an even more significant way that the pursuit of physical possessions distracts us. And most people never consider it.

## 3. Redirecting Our Focus

The third way in which our property and possessions distract us from our life goals is not as obvious or quantifiable as money and time. But it's just as real. In fact, it may be the most serious type of distraction—

by-stuff of all because it is so subtle. Stuff distracts us by obscuring our focus.

It's easy to see boxes in our closets or basements and recognize that we need to declutter. But when everyone around you is chasing more and more physical possessions, it starts to feel normal or expected, and it's harder to notice how that pursuit is distracting you from things that matter. The world around us will always seek to hijack our passions. Madison Avenue fills every unoccupied surface with messages of how its newest products will improve our lives. They call for our attention, our affection, and ultimately our admiration. And they are winning . . . more than we'd like to admit.

Before my wife and I became minimalists, a typical Sunday afternoon for us might include me lying on the couch and looking through the Best Buy ads. We had everything we needed and more. And yet, for some reason, I was compelled to see what was new, what was on sale, or what I could now afford to buy. When I say it aloud now, it sounds so foolish. *What a dumb way to spend my precious time—looking for things to buy when my house was already full of stuff not being used.* But at the time it seemed so normal, so expected. Everyone else was buying stuff, so surely this was the way to live.

Discovering minimalism changed that for me. While my wife and I have never described ourselves as extreme minimalists, living out of a backpack or moving into a two-hundred-square-foot tiny home, we did enter a quest to keep only what we needed to fulfill our greatest purposes and live according to our values. And along the way, we began to recognize the empty promises of consumerism and how the constant pursuit of more and more stuff detracts from our fullest potential.

Today, I'd much rather spend a Sunday afternoon playing tennis with my kids, hiking with friends, spending time with the neighbors, or even working on a book whose message will outlive me.

You've probably had a computer that glitched or slowed down because it had programs (maybe malware) running in the background. It became annoying and made you inefficient in your work. In the same way, materialism—thinking about what to buy, noticing what others have, watching TV shows about real estate and other purchases, daydreaming of what it would be like to live in that gated community you just drove by—takes up mental energy. Your distracted focus may not completely interfere with your pursuit of valuable goals, but like computer programs running in the background, it can slow you down. Who needs that? Life's short.

Minimalism is an investment in clarity. Mentally, it's the difference between a lantern and a laser beam.

Things that matter are usually challenging. If we're going to do them at our best, they require all we've got within us. Let's not give them second best—or worse, lose track of them altogether—by letting our minds dwell too much on things like sticks of furniture and threads of clothing.

Fortunately, whichever way our possessions are distracting us—by stealing our money, taking up our time, or obscuring our focus—the answer is the same: get rid of everything we don't need and then get on with our lives at a higher level of productivity. Minimizing takes effort, but on the other side of that effort is the ongoing payoff of greater freedom to accomplish the things we want.

## Less Shopping, More Living

Britt Bruce lives in Ontario, Canada, with her partner and a cross-eyed cat named Bacall. Britt recently decided to spend an entire year buying nothing—other than rent, food, and toiletries.

In some ways, her decision was a response to unhealthy shopping tendencies that she saw emerging in her life. "If there was something that was a 'good' deal and in my size," she told me, "I would probably end up buying it, even if I didn't totally love it or need it. It was on sale—how could I resist that? If I had to describe my online shopping habits in one word, it would be 'mindless.' And I knew something had to change."

But in another way, her self-imposed shopping ban was just a snap response to an unexpected car-repair bill. "I did the shopping ban to save money. I had just spent a small fortune on car repairs, and a ban on buying stuff seemed like it would be the easiest way to get my finances back on track."

A short-term decision, prompted by a crisis in finances, yielded life-changing results.

I first spoke with Britt about six months into her self-imposed experiment and asked her how it was going. The first thing she told me was that it was easier than she had thought it was going to be. "It shouldn't be difficult or controversial for someone to go six months without buying anything new. Maybe it sounds radical because we've been conditioned to believe we need new 'stuff' all the time. But really, we know that isn't the case. It's just clever marketing to convince us we need so much stuff."

Another early realization for Britt was how quickly the shopping ban sparked gratitude in her life. "Because I removed the option to go buy things to fill a void in my life, I actually started to notice all of the good stuff that I already did have in my life. I never felt like I didn't have exactly what I needed or I couldn't make it work with what I had."

By the end of the year, Britt was learning even more about herself.

"I learned how much of my life had been dictated by consumerism— the desire to buy something because it was new or shiny or my friends were buying it or sometimes just because it was on sale. I have become much more mindful of my shopping behavior. I only shop for something when I truly need it. And my shopping process today is more intentional, even considering an item for as long as possible before adding it to my cart."

More than that, as you can probably imagine, the newfound margin of time and money has allowed Britt to pursue new creative outlets that she didn't have time for before. "I've always enjoyed taking something that isn't living up to its fullest potential and giving it a makeover—whether that is clothes, art, electronics, or gardening. I love seeing items in this world flourish, and the shopping ban rekindled that passion inside me."

Can you see yourself in Britt's story? Even if you don't take on a yearlong shopping ban yourself, it's easy to see how the removal of pursuing physical possessions begins to teach us about ourselves and our greatest opportunities in the world.

## The Formula for Contentment with What You Own

So much of learning to pursue our big goals in life is about expanding our vision.

Just imagine what life would look like if you were content with what you had. What if you weren't scrolling Amazon, checking out the Kohl's sale, wanting a bigger house, or frequently upgrading clothes and other stuff? What if you were directing that passion toward things that matter?

The key to overcoming the passion for possessions, especially in a culture that normalizes that pursuit to such a degree, is contentment. There is an unmistakable freedom that accompanies contentment: a freedom to be who you are, enjoy who you are, and live the life you were destined to live. There are also health benefits to contentment. For example, it reduces your stress level, improves your outlook, relaxes your body, and makes life more enjoyable.[11] All good things and wonderful blessings.

The all-too-common life of over-owning possessions is a dense jungle that reduces our vision and slows our movements. A life of contentment with a simple material existence is a garden where all kinds of meaningful activities can grow and flower.

But how do we achieve contentment? We need to understand this. After all, I don't know a single person who doesn't desire it. It's just so elusive.

Let me offer an alternative approach to discovering this incredible blessing. The quickest way to find contentment is to start living with less.

---

## The quickest way to find contentment is to start living with less.

---

Many people think the opposite approach is the correct formula—once I want less, I will find it easier to own less. But for myself, and for countless others whom I have counseled on this pursuit, the correct starting place is to get rid of excess possessions. Once you do that, you'll *know* how little you need to live happily and productively, and then the desire for buying and owning will naturally fade.

**First own less, then want less.**

Try it. I think you'll find that's exactly how to discover contentment, slip out of the clutches of consumerism, and free yourself to accumulate a record of worthwhile accomplishments instead of a houseful of material goods.

## The Question You Should Be Asking About Your Possessions

A decluttering expert famously offered a question for deciding whether to keep a personal possession: "Does it spark joy?"

I've seen how this approach has prompted significant decluttering efforts, and I'm thankful to Marie Kondo for that. Yet I believe the question "Does it spark joy?" may not be as magical as it sounds and may actually rob tidying up of its fullest potential. "Sparking joy" is all about how things make us feel. It seems to accept that we will place our own happiness above everything else and that our possessions will help bring it about. Besides, many of the things we buy for our home, at one point or another, "sparked joy." That's why we bought them and struggle to part with them.

So let me propose an alternative question for us to ask ourselves when we're making the call on whether to hold or release any particular item in our possession. Rather than asking, "Does it spark joy?" let's ask, "Does it promote purpose?"

Is an item you're looking at, in some sense, a tool that contributes to your pursuit of the things that matter to you? For example, when you look into your overflowing closet, does having all those clothes help you fulfill your purpose? Or does it slow you down in the morning and make you feel burdened whenever you think of them? Would a streamlined wardrobe in an efficient closet be more likely to send you off on a day of accomplishments?

If you're a book collector, how many of those books on your shelves are you ever going to read again? Could it be that you're keeping them for decorative or sentimental, rather than practical, reasons? What if keeping far fewer books was a step toward creating a home office that is better at fostering your work on key projects?

Or what about all those boxes in your garage? Are they helping you efficiently store your car out of the elements? Or are they reminding you of the disorder and complications in your life every time you return to the house?

Your home is one of the most important places on earth to you, and it serves an important purpose in your life. Your home—whether it's two thousand square feet on six acres, eight hundred square feet in an apartment complex, or two hundred square feet on wheels—should be an environment that provides you an opportunity to rest, relax, and recharge. But it should also serve as a launching pad for your service in the world around you. Do the possessions in your home serve that purpose? Or has your home become so full of them that you're living life as merely a stuff manager rather than as a human being with goals and dreams, passions and purpose?

Unless your major life purposes require you to travel the world, living off the land, then you're going to need *some* possessions, such as *some* furniture, *some* kitchen utensils, *some* clothing. To maintain a connection with the past, we need *some* mementos and photos. And as we're creatures who are inspired and ennobled by beauty, we need *some* art and other lovely things about us.

These are necessities of life, and if you're going to fulfill your purposes, your needs have to be met. So it's important to note that owning less is not about owning nothing. It's about owning the right things—and the right number of them.

---

Owning less is not about owning
nothing. It's about owning the
right things—and the right
number of them.

---

You might even need to buy different or better things as your purposes change. For example, when I decided to become a writer, I needed new tools to accomplish that. I chose to buy high-quality computer equipment. This tech was an essential tool for my new purpose; I could neither skip it nor skimp on it. But I *could* afford it, because I saved money by getting rid of so much other burdensome stuff.

Still, my observation is that, for people living in Western and developed nations, nearly all of us should be focusing closely on getting rid of things. We own more than we need, and it is distracting us from our potential. So let's donate, recycle, or trash. It's said that the average American home contains three hundred thousand items.[12] How many can you get your house down to?

If you want more detailed help on how to own less, you can always read my book *The Minimalist Home: A Room-by-Room Guide to a Decluttered, Refocused Life.* But for now, the key decluttering question to keep in mind is, *Do these things promote my purpose?*

There's a big difference between tidying up your home and freeing up your life. Instead of merely sparking some joy within yourself, light a fire in the world.

## How Owning Less Begins to Change Us

Bonnie Balgeman is a thirty-eight-year-old respiratory therapist in south-central Montana. She's also the mother of two elementary-age sons and helps run the family ranch alongside her husband. Needless to say, she's a busy mom. But living with two boys on a ranch in Montana, she likes to say she's enjoying the season—and not just calving season.

Two years ago, she might not have said the same thing. A few years earlier, she and her husband moved into her grandparents' home, after their passing, to mind the ranch. "We moved into the small house, and everything they owned was still present, and we added our own,"

Bonnie said. "At the time, we had two healthy incomes and no kids, and I was a shopper. Needless to say, the stuff piled high. And when our boys were born, we just kept buying more and more."

That was until one morning, in the still of the dawn, when she had an epiphany that something needed to change in her home and life. "I was spending all my time managing the inventory of our home. I could barely keep up with the day-to-day activities of running a home for four, much less keep up with everything else in the house. It's like we were piling stuff on top of stuff, only to then have to move the piles to clean around the stuff. I had no time to simply enjoy my family. So I started to declutter and remove the possessions that weren't helping my family achieve their goals."

She tore through the lived-in areas of their home in about one month's time, although she is quick to add that adjusting and editing the possessions continues even today, two years later.

As Bonnie began decluttering, an important realization emerged in her thinking. "I started noticing all the things we were decluttering and the money that was spent on them. As I was placing things in donate piles, I could recall vividly purchasing the item. I saw myself at the register paying out the money for the item. Each time, I rationalized the purchase: 'This will improve my home and family's life.' And yet here I am, years later, and we never even used it. It was just stuff getting in the way of the time and energy I wanted to be spending with my kids."

Quickly, almost without warning, the process began changing her view of shopping in general. "I didn't need more to enjoy life," she said. "I needed less. I don't struggle with consumerism nearly as much as I used to. But when I do, I think of all the items I discarded, all the money wasted, all the time wasted, and all the energy I spent simply managing inventory. And I ask myself, *Is this really a thing I want to keep track of for the rest of my life?*"

I asked her how decluttering her possessions had changed her. This is what she said: "I live each day focused on the things that are important to me. Why would I ever go back to managing stuff that doesn't matter?"

This is how *owning* less leads to *wanting* less. This is how the act of decluttering our unneeded possessions removes us from the world of overconsumption we see all around us. And that is one of the reasons I am so passionate about minimalism and helping people experience its benefits. Once we see the advantages of owning less, it is a small step to experiencing contentment with our possessions.

As philosopher Alain de Botton put it, Jean-Jacques Rousseau believed that "there are two ways to make a man richer . . . : give him more money or curb his desires."[13] In my experience, the quickest way to curb our desires is to experience and appreciate the joy of living with less.

Those like Bonnie who choose to live with fewer possessions experience a dual benefit. First, owning fewer possessions frees up money, time, energy, and focus for the things that matter most. These people live with less stress, less distraction, and less environmental impact, and they become a better example for their kids and family. And second, those who choose to own less are quick to discover contentment and remove the pursuit of possessions from their lives. That is my story, and it can be yours as well.

Once you experience these benefits for yourself, it is easier to decipher the lies and artificial promises of a materialistic world.

Owning less leads to greater contentment. And greater contentment leads to the freedom to pursue things that matter.

# 8

## Trending

### Overcoming the Distraction of Applause

I think everybody should get rich and famous and do everything they ever dreamed of so they can see that it's not the answer.

—JIM CARREY

*Becoming Minimalist* made me think more than I ever had before about my deepest values and highest goals in life. For example, by freeing up our family finances, minimalism caused me to think about what I really wanted to do with my money. I realized I didn't want either money or possessions to distract me from the things that mattered to me. And in fact, in my own life, to one degree or another, I have had to face *all* the other distractions addressed in this book. But in this chapter, we come to the most serious distraction for me personally. You see, as the years go by, I care less and less about money and possessions . . . but the allure of others' applause for my achievements gets me every time.

Let me tell you about the time I realized the love of attention was a stumbling block for me, getting in the way of what I wanted to accomplish. This story is embarrassing to me, but I tell it because you may be able to relate in some way. It happened over several weeks early in 2014.

That time was a high point for me in several ways. On January 18, my book *Clutterfree with Kids* came out and then went on to spend two weeks as the number one parenting book on Amazon (without any algorithm-manipulating shenanigans). But that wasn't all. On the same day my book was released, the *Becoming Minimalist* Facebook page reached one hundred thousand fans—a major milestone. The *Becoming Minimalist* website had already reached one million visitors per month and was still growing.

It had been six years since I started my blog and three months since I switched careers to promote minimalism, and I believed I had made it. I felt like I was on top of the world.

I enjoyed it for about two weeks.

The fun came to an end when I was sitting at my dining room table and doing some work on my laptop. I began to notice some chatter on social media. Joshua Fields Millburn and Ryan Nicodemus, self-styled as the Minimalists, had been featured in an article on the home page of Yahoo. Around the same time I had published *Clutterfree,* they had published a book called *Everything That Remains,* and it, too, had done well in sales. The Yahoo News staff decided to feature them in an article about minimalism, and people in my social media world were congratulating them and praising them.

I knew and liked the Minimalists. We were working toward the same end—helping people live better lives by owning less. I should have been happy for them. But I wasn't.

Truth is, I was jealous. I thought, *It should be me getting the attention.*

It's a long and unsettling fall from the top of the world.

For one thing, it wasn't just about Joshua and Ryan. Later that same week, I noticed that another author's Facebook page was growing faster than mine. And then a different blogger's post was going viral. To make it worse, my book was no longer at the top of any bestseller lists. In fact, there were several parenting books selling better than mine. I began to regret that I hadn't titled my book *The 5 Love Languages to Expect When You're Expecting.*

Rather than celebrating one of the greatest seasons of my life, I had become petty and envious of the people around me. I wish I could say this was just a superficial jealousy that faded in the morning, but the envy was deeply rooted in my heart and I couldn't shake it, no matter what I tried.

Thankfully, within a few weeks, I was at a conference in San Diego listening to popular author Anne Lamott speak. During the question-and-answer period, someone got up from the audience and said, "What do I do about negative comments I get about my books?"

Lamott said (I'm paraphrasing here), "If you're hoping to find your self-worth and fulfillment in other people's opinion of you, you'll never find it."

Her statement caught my attention immediately. I thought back over the last several weeks and suddenly realized that was exactly what I had done. I had based my self-worth and happiness on the accolades I received from others. And as they began to turn elsewhere, so did my opinion of the life I was trying to live.

Finding our self-worth in recognition and approval from others is always a foolish pursuit. It negatively impacts the decisions we make and the lives we choose to live. Furthermore, applause never fully satisfies our hearts or souls. Even those who have reached the pinnacle of fame and prestige in our society long for more of the same. As the saying goes, you can never get enough of what you don't need to make you happy.

Our goal is not to secure approval from others. That is empty and fleeting. Our goal is to live the one life we've been given to its greatest potential—whether anybody praises us for it or not.

# The Sweet Odor of Praise

Praise is a tricky thing. It can be motivating, and you can use it to your benefit, but it can also cause you to lose your focus. To keep the applause coming, you may make decisions that detour you from a better path. Praise can easily become one of the reasons we might come to the end of our lives and regret that we never accomplished things that matter greatly to us.

Now, of course, not everybody is in the same position when it comes to the distraction of applause. Some of us have roles in society in which we naturally get more attention than others. Some of us are temperamentally more susceptible to letting praise go to our heads (here I have to raise my hand). Some of us have life goals that can benefit from lots of public recognition; others don't. But all of us need to be careful. The sound of applause is sweet, and it's addictive—we want more, more, more.

My grandfather used to say, "Praise is like perfume. Smell it, but don't swallow it." Maybe you're getting a lot (or *wishing* you were getting a lot) of praise for what you're doing in pursuit of your life goals. Then beware. It's so easy for the applause to replace the goals as your objective.

Or maybe it's just praise seeking in general that's causing you problems. One of the reasons people don't get around to pursuing the things and people that matter is that they're spending too much time trying to impress the boss or fuming over how little noticed they are or making TikTok dance videos they hope will go viral.

If you care about pursuing and accomplishing your life goals above all lesser occupations, you need to deal with the distractibility of applause. And the answer for too much applause is . . . more applause. Just not for you. I'll be getting to what I mean by that soon.

The goal is to make applause serve your purposes, not undermine them.

## Fame's Appeal

You've heard the phrase *fame and fortune*. Have you ever thought about the fact that fame comes first in that phrase? Could it be that human beings, at least many of us, are driven even more by the desire to be known and approved of than we are by the desire for wealth?

A social research study investigated the goals that tweens have. The top goal of all? Fame solely for the sake of being famous.[1] Maybe this is not surprising, given that this is a generation raised in the age of amateur YouTube stars, pop singers with Twitter followers in the tens of millions, and influencers who get to travel the world first class just because they look good in selfies.

But let's not pick on our kids. Many of us adults have a desire to be famous too. According to Orville Gilbert Brim, a social psychologist and author of *Look at Me! The Fame Motive from Childhood to Death*, about 30 percent of survey participants in Beijing and Germany—and over half in the United States—report daydreaming about being famous. In these three places, between 30 and 50 percent genuinely expect to acquire some degree of fame in their lifetime, if only for the proverbial fifteen minutes.[2]

Among adults, a desire for fame is usually tempered with a better understanding that fame has its downsides. And the hope of fame, or at least the expectation of it, tends to decline as we get older. Still, the attraction of having all eyes on us is powerful for many.

What's the appeal behind fame?

Research by psychologist Dara Greenwood and colleagues says that the number one reason people give for wanting to be famous is "*the desire to be seen/valued* (e.g., 'Being on the cover of a magazine,' 'Being recognized in public')."[3] As science reporter Benedict Carey put it in an article on the subject, "People with an overriding desire to be widely known to strangers are different from those who primarily covet wealth and influence. Their fame-seeking behavior appears rooted in a desire for social acceptance, a longing for the existential reassurance promised by wide renown."[4] Apparently there's a lot of emotional neediness out there. (But hey, who am I to talk?)

I hope you already know this, but let me just say it: You don't need praise or attention to have value. You have value just because you are you. But I get it—it's hard not to desire attention.

---

## You don't need praise or attention to have value.

---

The desire for applause has probably always been with the human race. The difference today is that media has made fame, or something resembling it, seemingly achievable by anyone. Everyone can put text, photos, music, or videos out there where (theoretically) anybody in the world can appreciate it. Multiple platforms are available for us to see how many people's attention we can grab with our viewpoints or self-expression. And in fact, numerous ordinary people have had their pictures or videos go viral almost by accident.

I've got news for you. Only about 0.0086 percent of the world's population is truly famous.[5] And that's just fine. Fame isn't all it's cracked up to be.

Of course, *some* applause is fine. *Some* applause is well earned. *Some* awards go to people who deserve recognition. If you're a leader, you can't have influence with your gift unless you have *some* followers.

But what is applause doing to you? Or if you're not getting much applause and you're bitter about it, what's your *desire* for applause doing to you?

The problem is, when we live for the applause of others—whether large scale or small scale—we begin to make sacrifices, and not healthy ones. We sacrifice our purpose, our values, or our focus.

In fact, could your desire for fame have influenced your choice of life goals in the first place? Maybe this is a chance to check and revise them. Maybe you need to be willing to do some things with your life that are never going to get much attention.

Whether the applause you're getting is related to your big life goals or to something else, it can distract you from the pursuits you've chosen. So here's the fix:

**Let yourself be smaller and others bigger.**

## Fame Versus the Dream

A resident of Lagos, Nigeria, Oluebube Princess Egbuna was a young woman who had a dream to be a software engineer. Early in her career, however, she became so well known within her field that others started looking to her for leadership and expertise. There was just one problem: she hadn't really advanced very far in the skills of software engineering.

Looking back, Egbuna sees clearly what led to the inconsistency. She was getting famous within the tech community as a software engineer, but she wasn't really a practicing software engineer at that time. She was advocating for inclusion and diversity in technology. This was getting her well known.

She began to feel like a fraud when others assumed she was a skilled software engineer and asked her questions in that field. She would have to put them off and go look up the answers on Google.

> As I got more famous, I got carried away and I completely forgot about my dream of being very good at software engineering. I was busy looking out for other

people, trying to protect my image as a presumed software engineer and mentor in tech. I was also teaching
things I didn't in reality practice. . . .
    I was simply distracted by fame![6]

It took a while, but eventually Egbuna spotted the problem and
acted on it. She was proud of being a diversity advocate, but it was
keeping her from what would really bring her fulfillment and enable
her to make a unique contribution.

Much later, I found myself and decided to dust off the effects of fame on myself and embrace what I truly wanted
to do. It was a journey! . . .
    My happily ever after is being a real software engineer
(what I really wanted to be) and also coming back to [be]
part of communities I really care about with no fame distractions.[7]

The sooner we recognize the perils of others' praise and approval,
the less damage is done.

## Building into Young Men

Back when I lived in New England, I had a friend who had long since
learned the importance of doing what matters, regardless of whether
it gained public attention or not. Jacob King, a former basketball and
rugby player, is now a father of three in Syracuse, New York, and an
international real estate developer. But I knew him for something
different—being a mentor to at-risk teenagers and being the founder
of a nonprofit organization supporting victims of domestic abuse.

Jacob grew up in Massachusetts in an unstable home but beat the odds to become a highly successful businessman in a couple of the world's superpowers.

"I spent more than a few nights in high school homeless," Jacob recalls. "Barely even graduated, in fact. Fortunately, there were a couple of teachers and guidance counselors who built into my life. One of them happened to teach honors Soviet studies at my high school. He invested in me, placed me in his class, and I was immediately hooked! I found the topic fascinating. When I went to college, I became a history major with a minor in Soviet studies—eventually studying Russian at Columbia University—traveling to and from the Soviet Union routinely."

After graduating from college, Jacob became a real estate investor and developer, dealing mostly in commercial office buildings, medical buildings, and apartments around Boston and throughout New England.

As his success in real estate at home grew, the Soviet Union began its collapse. In the early to mid-1990s, Russia became a major emerging real estate market.

"With my education, experience, and reputation, it was a natural step," Jacob told me. "There was a huge demand for Western-style commercial space, condos, and apartments. Investors from all over the world began entering the market, and both my expertise and language skills were attractive to them. So I became a consultant for heavyweight commercial investors and even considered moving my family to Moscow. Success stories and reputation were being added to my portfolio as quickly as square footage."

That was until Jacob had a conversation with a friend back home named Fred Walker. Jacob was discussing his success stories and opening up about a couple of failed projects. Fred said, "You know, Jacob, life is about more than amassing brick, mortar, and reputation."

Jacob immediately knew he was right. There were important things Jacob could accomplish with his life right where he was.

## Eight Things to Become Famous For

We're all going to be remembered for something, so we might as well aim to be known for all the right reasons. How about these?

1. *Kindness.* I have a good friend whom I once introduced to a neighbor. Shortly after their first meeting, my neighbor said to me, "Bob may be the kindest man I have ever met in my entire life." What an amazing compliment! Kindness—that is something I want to be known for.

2. *Perseverance.* At some point, everybody gets knocked down by life. Getting back up and remaining persistent in the face of trial—there's another trait worth being known for.

3. *Faithfulness.* To be known at the end of my life for being faithful to my wife, my kids, and my obligations is among my loftiest pursuits. I may be known for many things, but I'd trade them all to keep this reputation.

4. *Empathy.* Empathy is the ability to understand and share the feelings of another. And being known for it lays the foundation for countless good deeds in the lives of others—both in the lives of individuals and in society as a whole.

5. *Joy.* If you are known as the person who lights up a room and spreads genuine cheer wherever you go, you have reached an important level of fame.

6. *Encouraging.* An encourager, by default, cheers for the other person. Encouragers are not interested in winning at any cost. Quite the opposite—they want to see everyone win, and they work toward that end. As a result, they are beloved by many.

7. *Peacemaking.* If we need anything in this world today, we need more peacemakers. Blessed are you if you become one.

8. *Loving.* As the saying goes, "The greatest of these is love."[8] Become famous for loving others, and you'll never regret it.

His daughter had been diagnosed with type 1 diabetes a few years earlier, and he and his wife had taken in a boy, Brian, who was also diagnosed with it.

Jacob said, "So I immediately got involved supporting families and children with type 1 diabetes in my community and region. And I approached an existing local nonprofit about mentoring at-risk young men. My life was turned around by the investment of others, and I wanted to do the same. I knew my life's experiences could help provide a new perspective for someone going through something similar."

Jacob is one of the most generous men I've known. I've witnessed his impact on young men in his community, I've seen the support he provides for families dealing with the aftermath of abuse, and I've personally been molded into the man I am today in part because of our relationship and conversations.

As I like to tell him, he went from building skyscrapers in Moscow to building into the lives of others. And it wasn't for the sake of reputation or fame. In fact, before reading this story, you'd probably never heard of him. But there are countless lives being touched by the life he has chosen to live.

## Turning the Spotlight

I went to college with a guy named Chris Saub. He was a talented musician (and still is), and he could have been obsessed with how much people were appreciating his artistry. But that wasn't his way. Or, because the music business is highly competitive, he could have taken a very me-centered approach to fame and praise, but he was very different from that.

What struck me most about Chris was how encouraging this guy was to others. If another student got a job, I swear Chris would be more excited than the newly employed student. "Are you kidding, that's great! Congratulations! I'm so happy for you. You deserve it, and I'm sure you're going to do great. Wow! That's just so cool."

Or if a fellow musician got a recording deal, Chris didn't act anything like I did when the Minimalists were getting more public attention than I was. He'd be so happy for the other musician. "That's amazing! Good for you. This is going to be so great for your career! I can't wait until the recording comes out. I'm going to tell everybody about this."

I once asked Chris why he got so excited for others' success. I'll never forget the advice he gave me: "No one else's glory can take away from yours. And vice versa."

He continued, "Life isn't a game of musical chairs where you have to be the first to sit down to enjoy the prize. There are enough chairs for everyone. When I see someone have success, I'm happy for them. It's exciting to see someone take a step or reach a milestone in their life. It inspires me to do the same."

Back in college, I was already struggling with my desire for accolades and my jealousy toward people who seemed to be succeeding beyond me. So Chris's selfless pleasure in other people's achievements stunned and impressed me. I remember his enthusiasm for others even twenty-five years later. It's a quality I've always wanted more of in my life.

Another time, back when I was a youth pastor, I was at a conference with a bunch of other youth pastors. The group leader asked, "What brings you the most joy?"

I said, "When I'm up front teaching." Teaching is one of the main responsibilities of a youth pastor, and I had a passion to do it well. It is one of the most important things we can do for students who are forming their views on life, morality, and faith. Also, the attention I got for my teaching made me feel good about myself, more confident, more ready to do my best in my job. So I thought my answer was a good one.

Then someone further down the line answered the question "What brings you the most joy?" this way: "When I'm watching my intern up front teaching."

Ouch.

I don't think the other youth pastor said this to spite me. But his answer struck me as an entirely different way to see the world. This guy was focused on handing off responsibility and attention to others and rooting for them to be a success.

Who had a healthier attitude: the other youth pastor or me? Whose approach would produce more good work in the long run: his or mine?

As I said, one solution to the distraction of applause is . . . more applause. Applause for others. Don't worry so much about the extent of your own reputation. Build up the reputations of other worthy people.

---

## Don't worry so much about the extent of your own reputation. Build up the reputations of other worthy people.

---

Are you working at a nonprofit with a team as one of your major life goals? Good for you. Just make sure the praise for the good works gets appropriately spread around so that everyone gets a healthy amount and no one gets too much. And see that the work is what gets promoted, not you.

Have you and your spouse decided to provide foster care to kids with troubled backgrounds? That's important work and far from easy, so you deserve a lot of credit. But your spouse is right in there with you in this service, right? If others go overboard in praising you, do you redirect some of that praise to your spouse?

Try working phrases like these into your speech:

- "I couldn't have done it without X."
- "It's a team effort, and we've got a great team."
- "You should get Y to tell you that story."

Does this seem hard to you? Even if you're a leader, being the center of attention may not be as important to your success as you think. Chinese philosopher Lao-tzu is often credited as saying, "A leader is best when people barely know that he exists. . . . Fail to honor people, they fail to honor you. But of a good leader, who talks little, when his work is done, his aims fulfilled, they will all say, 'We did this ourselves.'"

Before I become guilty of saying, "I did this myself," let me give credit where it is due.

I've given credit to minimalism for the things I've been able to accomplish. But I must give at least as much credit to my wife, Kim. She is a supportive wife and loving mother. She handles all the kids' schedules and school prep. She allows me to do my work because of our partnership.

Considering how much I owe her, I feel even more foolish of becoming jealous of the Minimalists. After all, I wouldn't have accomplished half the things I have if it weren't for Kim's selflessness and abilities. And yet she gets far less attention than I do.

We overcome desire for personal accolades by learning to encourage and cheer on others. As nineteenth-century American orator Robert Ingersoll said, a "superior" person "rises by lifting others."⁹

We can celebrate the achievements of others. And if they start taking the accolades that we wish we had received, that's okay. We can still have the satisfaction of knowing we had a role in promoting worthy people and their causes.

# Two Questions to Ask Yourself About Your Social Media Activity

So many of us today are tempted by fleeting social media fame. We desire "likes" and "retweets" and "comments" and "views" and "clicks." We refresh our Instagram or Facebook page minutes after posting a photo or status update just to see how many other people have clicked a heart or thumbs-up.

You don't have to be on social media to make a difference in the world, but if you're like me, you need social media to promote your cause. Some people can take a "fast" from social media to break its psychological hold on them; others don't have that luxury. The temptations that come with social media are always there for them.

What do you do?

Two simple questions can help you straighten out your motives and behaviors in the use of social media.

1. *Why* am I attracting followers?

Are you trying to be famous? To get rich? To meet an emotional need within yourself?

Or is it to communicate with friends and like-minded others? Perhaps to earn some social currency you can use for the benefit of the people and causes you care about?

Your motives may never be absolutely pure, nor even entirely knowable to yourself, but if you're conscious of them, you can also consciously keep your social media behavior in line with your intentions.

2. *How* am I attracting followers?

The internet is full of meaningless content from people, websites, and channels just trying to get clicks and likes. It is also full of content designed only to stir up unhealthy emotional responses. There are a whole lot of undesirable ways to attract followers on social media.

Are you attracting followers with dignity? Integrity? Truth? Consistency? Substance?

What are your standards in social media posting? Perhaps you need to come up with a set of guidelines for yourself. Turn your social media activity toward good, even if it means having fewer followers.

This will keep you on message.

## Focused on the Real Prize

If you're like me and there are times when you get sidelined because you're fixated on how the praise you're getting isn't enough, then I have two hopeful thoughts for you.

First, it gets easier.

The more focused on and committed to your goals you become, the less an excessive hunger for others' applause should trouble you. When you're doing what you know you're supposed to be doing, it starves the wolf of envy within you.

When I had some extra money a number of years ago, I chose to use it to start the Hope Effect. That was a high priority for me then, and it still is now. I'm still devoting my time and financial resources to this cause.

So when a friend uses his extra money to buy a Corvette, I can compliment him on his car without wishing I had one myself. I've got something better. And every time I go to one of our foster care sites, I see it in the eyes of boys and girls who lost their parents but are happy, healthy, and full of hope.

Do I still struggle with too much desire for accolades? I sure do. But I can honestly say that it's not the big issue it used to be. It doesn't hold me back in my pursuit of the things that matter to me.

A desire for attention doesn't have to hold you back either.

Accept deserved praise graciously. Redirect praise to others generously. And never lose sight of your mission, no matter how much or how little limelight is shining on you.

And now I'll give you the second encouraging thought to take with you: people are attracted to others who are living their mission.

---

## People are attracted to others who are living their mission.

---

A mom is devoted to raising her four kids, and the neighbors see it. A woman from down the street calls to say, "I've got a problem with my son, and if you don't mind, I'd like to hear how you would handle the same thing with your boys."

A competent worker gets noticed by the new intern who just started.

A great coach is appreciated by his players.

A gifted backup singer may be known within her industry.

A great listener is the first phone call of a friend in despair.

Focusing on living your mission may never make you famous (which is about you). But it can make you influential (which is about others).

Aim for the purpose and not the praise.

I'd applaud you for doing that, but I wouldn't want it to distract you.

# 9

## Beaches Get Boring

### Overcoming the Distraction of Leisure

Instead of wondering when your next vacation is, maybe
you should set up a life you don't need to escape from.

—SETH GODIN, *TRIBES*

I tend to be a driven person—someone who wants to achieve and succeed. Yet I don't think I come off to most people who know me as intense, hurried, or obsessed, the sort of person who runs over other people. In fact, probably the opposite: I'm known for being calm and peaceful, focused and attentive. That's because not only do I love to work by nature, but I also love the work that I do: helping others live more intentional lives through owning less. I can relax and feel at home in my work.

If I wake up before the rest of my family on a Saturday morning, most likely I'll get a cup of coffee and drift over to my laptop, where I'll put in some time answering people's questions about minimalism that I receive via email. I don't *have* to—it could wait till Monday. But I *want* to. That's because (to put it as Seth Godin does) I have my work life set up in such a way that I don't want to escape from it. Instead, I'm drawn toward it because I love it.

Certainly I realize that not everybody has the same kind of personality I do. (Thank the Lord for variety.) Furthermore, I fully realize that work looks different from one person to another. We have a huge range of jobs, professions, and enterprises, and some of us are more comfortable in certain ones than others.

Nevertheless, I believe that for just about everybody, the most fulfilling thing we can do, in the long term, is to focus on our work. By "work," I'm not just referring to a nine-to-five job. It could be parenting. Or serving on a board. Or volunteering. Many possible things. Anything that contributes good to others is *work*, regardless if we're getting paid for it.

And what distracts us most from that kind of work? One of the biggest things is work's opposite: leisure. Or better put, modern society's infatuation with leisure.

Before you think I'm someone who wants to talk you out of your hobby and would hide the keys to your RV if I could, I need to tell you that my family and I take two extended vacations every year, once in the summer and once at Christmastime. I regularly take time off from work to pick up my daughter from school, attend my son's sports activities, or have a lunch date with the beautiful Mrs. Becker. My week has a healthy rhythm to it because I've taken the advice of a former mentor who said, "You should take two days off each week—one to take care of house duties and one when you rest as much as possible."

So I'm *not* against rest, relaxation, and fun. I just don't want you to miss out on the things that matter to you because you've unthinkingly bought into our cultural notions of leisure. What I'm against is making leisure your *objective*. Because if leisure is your objective, it will inevitably displace your higher priorities. That's a very common problem in our society.

Let me put it this way: Leisure makes a great booster to long-term productivity in our pursuit of meaningful goals. But leisure makes a terrible goal in itself.

# Leisure makes a great booster to long-term productivity in our pursuit of meaningful goals. But leisure makes a terrible goal in itself.

Leisure doesn't provide meaning. It provides renewal for other things that do provide meaning.

The people I've known who have made leisure their purpose have tended to feel empty and have eventually regretted what they gave up for leisure. They get bored with sunbathing at the beach, playing golf, or watching TV. I don't want you or me to end up the same way.

In our society, leisure becomes a distraction primarily in two ways:

- We tend to see work as a necessary evil and try to get away with doing as little of it as possible.
- We assume we should stop working at a certain age, and usually we hope that age is as early in life as we and our retirement savings can make it.

To understand this better, we have to start by looking more closely at what our work means to us.

## Why We Work

It may not be entirely historically accurate, but I picture a time when families were responsible for accomplishing everything for their existence: hunt, farm, build, sew, cook, clean, and so on. Until one day when somebody noticed his or her family was better at farming than building and decided to barter with a neighboring family. "If we grow extra food and give it to you, will you build an extra house that we can live in?"

Division of labor was born. Both benefited from the arrangement: better food was grown and stronger homes were built. In the end, all of society benefited. And each individual was able to pursue contribution to the community in his or her area of giftedness and passion, whether that be farming, building, sewing, hunting, or fishing.

But somewhere along the way, we lost our focus on how work benefits everyone. We no longer worked to benefit others but rather to benefit ourselves. Work became selfish. Work became that thing through which we make money so that we can do the other things we really want to do.

Dorothy Sayers (best known as the creator of the Lord Wimsey mysteries) said in an essay on work,

> What I urged then was a thoroughgoing revolution in our whole attitude to work. I asked that it should be looked upon—not as a necessary drudgery to be undergone for the purpose of making money, but as a way of life in which the nature of man should find its proper exercise and delight and so fulfill itself to the glory of God. . . .
>
> The habit of thinking about work as something one does to make money is so ingrained in us that we can scarcely imagine what a revolutionary change it would be to think about it instead in terms of the work done.[1]

Sayers wrote that more than eighty years ago, during World War II, and her sentiment is truer now than ever. Work today is widely seen as an exercise in making money or as something to avoid and shortcut if possible.

In the Things That Matter Survey, we asked, "Which is a more attractive goal: to retire early and live a life of leisure or to work a long
time at a job you find fulfilling and productive?" Only about a third
of respondents (34 percent) see working a fulfilling job as more attractive than retiring early to live a life of leisure. It seems many of us are
working more because we have to than because we want to.

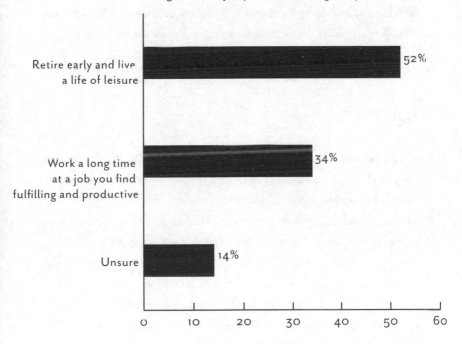

Which is a more attractive goal: to retire early and live a life of leisure
or to work a long time at a job you find fulfilling and productive?

In its 2017 *State of the Global Workplace* report, the Gallup polling
organization revealed that just 15 percent of employees worldwide are
engaged in their job, while 67 percent are not engaged, and 18 percent are actively disengaged. The highest levels of engagement are
found in the United States and Canada, though at 31 percent, that
still leaves more than two-thirds disengaged. Australia/New Zealand

and Western Europe trail considerably, with 14 percent and 10 percent engagement, respectively.[2]

It can't be that 85 percent of jobs worldwide are bad. There is something else contributing to this amount of disengagement at work.

I believe it relates to how we view work. The reason 85 percent of us are disengaged at work is because we're thinking about it all wrong. We see it as the thing we do to make the money so we can buy the house or take the vacation. Work, in this way, has become entirely selfish.

Work is what I do so I can get the money to do the things I want to do. With that as the mindset, no wonder we focus so much on leisure: the weekend, holidays, vacation, and retirement.

## Leisure Bait

We like our time off from the job. You could almost say we're obsessed with it. A lot of us claim we're "working for the weekend." Monday is the butt of countless jokes. Wednesday is called "Hump Day" because it puts us on the downward slope to the weekend. And we print mugs, T-shirts, and magnets proclaiming, "Thank God it's Friday."

Too many people waste their weekdays by always wishing for the weekend, exalting Saturday and Sunday over Monday and Tuesday. Those who learn to love and make the most of every day are less likely to look back and realize they've wished and wasted their lives away. Yet we just go on valuing our time off more than our time on.

In the United States, 40 percent of the time when workers "call in sick," they're faking.[3] The average American spends nearly two hundred hours a year—the equivalent of twenty-five working days!—daydreaming about vacations.[4]

But there's an irony here.

We're so devoted to our work that it impinges on our days off. A little more than half of US workers do not use all their paid vacation time. A similar percentage (over 50 percent) report feeling guilty about taking vacation time.[5]

While on vacation, many Americans never really get away from their workplace. Seventy percent of vacationing US workers check in with their workplace at least occasionally. Furthermore, 30 percent check in at least once a day, and about 11 percent do so several times a day.[6]

Do we really *need* to do this? Or are we so addicted to the daily grind that we can't do without it even on our long-anticipated vacations? Have we invested so much of our sense of self-worth in our jobs that we can't spend a week at the beach or ten days exploring the Canadian Rockies without reverting to our jobs to stroke our egos?

We care about our time off both *too much* and *not enough*. On the one hand, we think of time off as the destination we're slogging through our workdays to get to. On the other hand, we don't take advantage of our time off to really rest and become refreshed.

What is with these conflicting realities? Is this odd tension because we're misunderstanding the role of rest? Are we seeing the goal of work to be rest, rather than recognizing that the goal of rest is accomplishing better work?

We've got everything flipped upside down, and it's leading to this confusion.

The goal of work isn't more rest. The goal of rest is better work.

---

## The goal of work isn't more rest. The goal of rest is better work.

---

I don't work hard so I can vacation well. I vacation well so I can work better. It's a different way of seeing what the motivation is.

Take your weekends, personal days, and holidays off. And take at least one extended vacation per year. If you can't afford to go far or do anything exotic, that's fine. You can still disconnect from work. And really rest. Have fun.

Get some distance from your work, not as an escape, but so that you can get some perspective on it. Recharge so that you can be your best self and do your best work when you get back.

R&R is not enough. We need R&R&R—*rest* and *relaxation* and an enthusiastic *return to work*.

## Inventing Retirement

In our society, there's not just an ongoing propensity to take life easy and enjoy but also an end goal of eliminating work from your life entirely so you can finally "enjoy retirement." Among the generations that staff the workplace today, there's a trend toward wanting to retire earlier and earlier.[7]

Is this good? Or is it bad?

My grandfather Harold Salem had a lot to say about retirement. One of the things he used to tell me was "Retirement was invented by the politicians, and that should tell you everything you need to know about it."

I used to wonder if that was really true. So I started to research the history of retirement. And you know what? He was totally right!

Retirement is basically a modern experiment. In generations past, everyone kept working as long as they were physically able. Historians say that Otto von Bismarck, chancellor of Germany, had a hand in inventing the modern concept of retirement in 1883 when he offered a pension to any nonworking German over the age of seventy, which was lowered to sixty-five a few years later. Other nations, including the United States, followed suit.[8]

In other words, sixty-five was an arbitrary age set by politicians to garner votes. Then, somewhere along the way, that particular age became the gold standard for retirement, even though it had nothing to do with the best approach to living the most meaningful life for the individual.

So, if retirement is an experiment, how's it going? I would say, not so well.

Preparing financially for retirement creates a great deal of angst. Just notice how many financial retirement commercials there are. Or how much mental energy you put into thinking about your retirement accounts. People are busy calculating how soon they can retire and worrying that they won't have enough. And if a stock market correction comes along and miniaturizes pre-retirees' nest eggs, it's considered a terrible shame that they might have to work a couple more years before retiring. (Could it be a blessing instead?)

Do you know what the biggest unintended consequence of this focus on retirement is? It takes away the joy of the job. Why? Because how will we learn to enjoy work if our goal is to get out of it as soon as possible? We work so we can stop working rather than working because it is meaningful to us.

Additionally, there's a mindset among most people that retiring (probably around the age of sixty-five) is the only way to go. And thus, masses of people have retired when they didn't really need to, leaving positions where they were still able to contribute much to society and get the satisfaction that comes from it.

So is retirement really as great as we think it is? Or is it causing us to miss out on things that actually matter and things we can be proud of when we get to the ends of our lives?

## Not Retiring but Retooling

If you're presuming that you must retire, I dare you to reconsider. How much is the cultural attitude toward retirement affecting your view of work or the goal of your work? The very word *retire* means to go away, to leave the center of action. Who wants that? Especially when you have so much good left to give.

My grandpa said, "I want to retire three days before my funeral." (He almost made it, too—he worked forty hours per week until nine days before his death, at age ninety-nine!) He always credited work as one of the reasons why he stayed mentally sharp. And I know it's one of the reasons he could face death with such confidence—he didn't waste a single year of his life.

Of course, age is a real factor in our work, sometimes making aspects of our work harder for us. But as you age, you might choose not to *retire* from your career but to *retool* it. For example:

- You might slow down, going from full-time to part-time or seasonal work.
- You might switch to less physically demanding work.
- You might do more advising than leading, moving into a mentorship role.
- You might change to a different field or type of job, perhaps one that aligns more closely with your life goals, even though it may pay less.

Eventually, however, you might choose to retire from paid employment altogether. It's not always wrong. Sometimes it's the best choice to bring your job to a conclusion, especially if you're planning on focusing more on the causes you care about while in retirement.

In our youth-focused society, I wish we could recover a better appreciation for age. It's not only about younger people looking more often to older people for advice; older people themselves could have a higher view of what they can offer others. In your later years, you have much to contribute, probably more than ever. The best fruit grows on the most mature trees.

Research shows that retirement from typical employment, when undertaken in the right way, can improve both health and life satisfaction.[9] Yet 28 percent of recent retirees find that life is worse than when they were working. They feel a sense of "isolation and a loss of direction."[10] So how do the other 72 percent find happiness in retirement?

Stephen Wright, a financial advisor, put it well: "The key to a happy retirement is to have something that you are retiring *to*, not just something that you are retiring *from*. The difference between happy and unhappy retirees is having a purpose."[11] In other words, keep contributing. "Work" doesn't have to include a paycheck every two weeks—it might be something meaningful like helping to raise a grandchild or volunteering more hours in your community.

Don't retire until you really need to. And if you do retire, retire with a purpose.

---

## If you do retire, retire with a purpose.

---

Whatever your worker status, take stock of the years you might have left and renew your commitment to your top goals. As long as you've got breath, keep contributing positively to the world around you.

## Geezer Power

Omaha native Paul Stratman spent forty-four years in the electrical trade, laying wire, managing people, and eventually doing 3D modeling. Then he retired.

Dissatisfaction soon set in. "My wife had a long list of things she wanted done around the house," Paul said, "but that took me less than a year to complete. And I certainly didn't want to just sit around the house doing nothing for the rest of my life. I wanted to help people."

About this time, he heard about a group of retired tradesmen in the Omaha area who call themselves the Geezers. Several times each week, for a half day at a time, a group of five to ten Geezers meets in North Omaha (a poorer part of town) to rebuild a house for later use by a nonprofit.

"Currently, we're rebuilding a home that will house six former inmates," Paul told me. "We're providing the home, and the nonprofit will provide the mentorship when the gentlemen move in."

The goal is to help formerly incarcerated people build better lives and stay out of jail. The rate of recidivism in the United States reaches as high as 83 percent.[12] "Our goal is zero percent among the men who will occupy this home when we are finished," Paul said.

On a previous occasion, after the devastating 2019 midwestern floods, Paul was working as a volunteer in the area to restore electricity to many of the homes when he received an urgent phone call concerning a couple in their fifties whose home had been destroyed in the flood. The couple were living in a camper with their teenage daughter and three grandkids (whose mother was unable to take care of them) while they tried to get enough money to fix their house. Six people in a tiny camper! The couple were worried because they had been informed that someone from Nebraska's Division of Children and Family Services would be coming to inspect the living conditions for the three grandkids. The couple feared their grandkids were going to be taken from them. They were almost frantic to prevent that. Would Paul help?

Paul went right to work. He completed the electrical wiring and safety renovations inside the flood-damaged home, free of charge, in time for it to pass inspection by CFS. The family stayed together.

Reflecting on this experience, Paul said, "When you can help people that are so desperate, and can make a little difference in their lives—people who have put their lives on hold to care for the needs of someone else—it is moving. That was one of the most emotional experiences I've ever had and some of the most meaningful work I've ever accomplished." Paul has retired from his job, but he hasn't stopped working for others.

## Many Happy Returns

Several years back, I met a woman named Theresa. She was seventy and thin, with a sweetness of nature you noticed right away. Talking to her, I discovered we had some things in common when she mentioned that she was a CPA. (I had studied some accounting in college.) She was retired by the time I knew her, but I was fascinated to learn that she was still putting her education and expertise to good use. From January to April—that is, in the run-up to Tax Day—she would go to downtown Phoenix every weekday and help low-income women prepare their tax returns, all without charging a fee.

"I explain and work to make sure the women get all the resources that the government has provided for them," she explained to me, her face lighting up. "I've spent my life helping businesses do the same. Now I appreciate helping the disadvantaged. Many of them can't read, much less fill out a complicated tax form.

"I've spent decades studying the tax code, and I'm putting that knowledge to good use now in retirement."

## A Necessary Good

We need a different view of work. It's not a necessary evil. It's not something that's possibly interesting for a while when we're young adults but then something we're bound to get tired of later as we start shirking or looking for the exit.

The truth is, the world needs your talents and abilities. We need you to work hard and do it well. Your work contributes to the good of society and moves us forward. Your contribution makes us better as people. It enriches our lives.

Whether you are bagging groceries, delivering mail, sweeping streets, parenting children, or managing others, you can view your hard work as an act of love to the people you serve. And when you change your motivation, you'll discover that work is not something to be avoided—it is meaningful and rewarding. Monday is not a day to be dreaded.

Please don't view your work as something only to be endured or escaped. Instead, rethink your work. Regain focus and motivation to use your passions and abilities to contribute good to a society in need of them. Your work is a way of showing love to others.

### Love your work because your work is love.

## Beyond the Paycheck

The Things That Matter Survey asked, "Do you find fulfillment in your career/work beyond a paycheck?" About half—53 percent—said yes. No: 31 percent. Unsure: 17 percent.

It is time for *all* of us to begin redefining work and finding fulfillment outside the paycheck. Not because your employer offers a great vacation package or a parking spot close to the building, but because

Do you find fulfillment in your career/work beyond a paycheck?

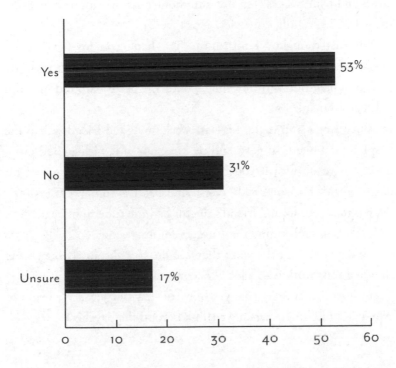

your work improves life for everyone. You do what you do well, whether you are paid or not, so that someone else can go do what they do well, and everyone benefits. That's why I call work *love.*

Sometimes this love takes the form of building a strong, more affordable home. Sometimes it's farming better food or sewing better clothes. Other times it's cleaning someone's teeth, helping with their taxes, mowing their lawn, or working as a grocery store clerk to collect money that can be paid to farmers for their next round of crops.

Regardless of what your job is, in almost every circumstance, you are bringing a benefit to society. And when we start to see our jobs in this way, we instantly find more joy in them.

I remember sharing this idea of work with a roomful of several hundred people. A young man approached me afterward and said, "I like what you had to say about work. But I'm a landscaper. I mow lawns and trim bushes. I'm not sure how much my job is benefiting the world. I certainly don't view it as love."

"My first thought," I told him, "is 'Thank you for making my neighborhood beautiful.' Every time I go for a run, a walk with my wife, or a bike ride with my son, I enjoy the beauty around me. You did that, so thank you.

"But I won't stop there. Just last week, my good friend was in the hospital for a major surgery, and he came out of it with a good prognosis. I have no idea if you're the landscaper who takes care of his doctor's yard, but somebody does. And because somebody is doing the job that you do, my friend's doctor had the time to offer his gifts and talents in performing that surgery for my friend.

"So thank you for the work that you do. It is absolutely benefiting all of us. Your work feels a lot like love to me."

See how this entirely changes how we view our jobs? We begin to experience fulfillment when we think beyond the paycheck.

## A Therapeutic Change

Mark Mahnensmith is a father of four—two sets of twins—living in Rhode Island. He is a physical therapist and loves his job, not just because he loves the work or the people or the company, but also because he sees his work as love.

It wasn't always this way for Mark. After college, Mark chose a career in finance, going to work at one of the largest investment banks on Wall Street. He was making lots of money and began envisioning himself retiring at age thirty-five.

"At the time," he told me, "I didn't care what work I was doing. I just wanted to make a lot of money. But I began to notice something in my life. I couldn't fall asleep at night, and I couldn't wake up in the morning. Something needed to change."

He began to reminisce as he shared his story. "I was an athlete in high school and was always good at pushing myself harder than others and getting more out of my body. I wanted to help others do the same with theirs. So I went back to school to become a physical therapist. It was a career that would allow me to live the family life that I wanted, but more than that, it would allow me to love and serve others through my giftedness and passion."

Mark has been a physical therapist for the last ten years and is much happier now. In his own words, "Not because there was anything wrong with investment banking, but because I see work differently now. And I see my role in the world, through the job that I do, differently."

He continued, "I don't see my work as just a job that pays our bills. I see it as an opportunity to connect with people. In fact, I receive my greatest satisfaction when I help someone learn about their physical body or I can simplify a process for them that changes their mindset or outlook. My career helps other people be their best selves, and that is one of the most loving things any of us can do for another."

It's important to note, in Mark's story, that he does not speak ill of bankers or the financial industry. In fact, when I talked to him about his career change (I first met Mark when he was in school to become a physical therapist fifteen years ago), he believed that if he had viewed his previous work differently, he could have approached it as a work of love too.

There are very few jobs in the world today that are not service to others. The investment banker, the physical therapist, the volunteer teacher's aide, the garbage collector, the insurance salesperson, the pro bono paralegal, the highway construction worker, the landscaper—

each of them improves the quality of life for others and allows them to be their best selves. It all comes down to how we view our work.

## What a Way to Make a Living

When I published my first book with a traditional publisher—a book titled *The More of Less*—one of the cover designer's first mock-ups showed a lounge chair on a beach. My reaction? No, no, no! This was exactly the opposite of the impression I wanted to give. I have never pursued minimalism as a means to check out of my obligations and opportunities, and I didn't want the cover to reflect that common misconception. The point of minimalism (the topic of the book) for me is not to move quicker to the point where we don't have to do anything. It's to make us *more* productive. We remove distractions so we can live our best lives of contribution to others.

I want to close this chapter with an important truth: your most meaningful and fulfilled life will include hard work. They are connected and correlated. As human beings, we are designed to work not for the sake of money, possessions, or fame but because it is in our nature to live up to our fullest potential through accomplishing good for those around us. And so your most meaningful pursuits will not be easy; they will require focus and effort.

Now, just to be clear, I am not advocating being busy just to be busy. I am advocating for the importance of doing your work (whether paid or unpaid) in a focused and deliberate way, putting your whole self into it—doing the best you can to accomplish the most you can with the one life you've got.

I spoke at an event in Iowa years ago on the importance of work and the life-giving fulfillment that comes from it. A woman pulled me aside afterward to share a story with me.

"I own a small restaurant in my hometown," she started. "Last

Mother's Day, I was short on staff and hired a teenage girl to help us clear tables that day. It was one of the busiest days of the year—Mother's Day always is. At the end of the day, I looked over at the young girl. She was sitting on a stool near the dishwasher. I approached her and commented on how crazy the day was. She replied to me, 'I am absolutely exhausted. I don't think I've ever felt this tired before in my life.'"

The woman sharing the story looked me in the eyes and continued: "I looked at her and said, 'I know. Doesn't it feel great?'"

Just like everyone else, I enjoy a day off. I love waking up slowly and cooking a leisurely breakfast for my family. I enjoy reading a book, playing pickup basketball at the local park, or watching a movie with my kids. And I appreciate vacations, whether we're heading back over Christmas to see extended family or enjoying a ski trip together over spring break. Those are days I look forward to.

But nothing beats the feeling of laying my head on the pillow at the end of a day of meaningful work and knowing that I gave everything I had to the day. As the restaurant owner said, it really does feel great. When I get to the end of my life, I will want to know that I tried my best and gave my all. So will you.

The way to overcome the distraction of leisure is to rethink it and find selfless fulfillment in work. If you have a job, see it as love by serving others. If your days are spent in parenting and housework, see that as love. Even if you are unemployed and have way too much time on your hands, there is still meaningful service to others you can find to do.

---

The way to overcome the distraction of leisure is to rethink it and find selfless fulfillment in work.

I know that work is messy and never perfect. And even if the good you are designed to bring into the world is the job that you are paid to do, there are still hard days, hard relationships, and hard things that you have to accomplish that you might not always be happy to do. But if you're working on things that matter, you'll never regret it.

# 10

## Blinking Lights
### *Overcoming the Distraction of Technology*

Right before you die, you'll realize your whole life was
about loving people. And you watched too much television.

—DONALD MILLER

*Becoming Minimalist* started as a blog back in the days when blogging
was young and I barely knew what I was doing. Later, I started posting
to Facebook and Twitter when bored one evening, and I started to
observe what kinds of messages gained followers on these platforms
and how they could be used to spread the message of minimalism. *Oh,
that's how all this works,* I remember thinking to myself. To be honest,
it was simply a process of stumbling into technology. An app, a couple
of online magazines, and untold numbers of livestream videos later,
and one thing is clear to me: without modern technology, I would
never have been able to fulfill my goal of promoting minimalism with
anything like the reach that I now have.

Still, there are times when technology doesn't help me but rather
gets in the way of my living out my purposes and values. As alert to
this problem as I am, I still frequently catch myself wasting time on
social media or reading a news story that is irrelevant to me. I have to

remind myself again and again to click the red Close button or turn my phone facedown.

If ever there was something that deserved the label *distraction,* it's the electronic news, entertainment, information, and time-consuming games that modern technology pushes in our direction. (Not that we put up much of a resistance most of the time.) All those blinking lights and colorful icons and entrancing sounds—they're hard to ignore. Technology can quickly move from tool to distraction when we're not careful. In the end, it can lead to regret.

## The New Triviality

Long before we were bitten in the neck by FAANG (Facebook, Apple, Amazon, Netflix, Google), human beings had a penchant for engaging with the trivial in place of the important. I imagine people used to spend too much time listening to programs on their giant living room radios, or handing over their coins at the nickelodeon theater, or hanging out at the pool hall. Go back even further, and I'm sure people got caught up in jousting—or chariot racing—more than was good for them. In fact, I read an essay in college written two thousand years ago (during the Roman Empire) arguing against the foolishness of wasting your days at the Colosseum watching the gladiators.

At least in the old days we used to have to excuse ourselves to entertain the trivial. We left home to go to the corner bar, or we took an afternoon off work to catch a ball game. When I was a kid, we would go to the basement to play video games, because that's where the gaming devices were wired to our TV. Nowadays, I can pull out my phone anywhere at any time—at the dinner table, on a date with my wife, at my son's soccer game. The distractions from things and people that matter (often sitting right in front of us) are present to a new degree.

Today, much of our leisure activity has migrated out of the real world and onto our devices, making the distraction of the trivial ever present. Many of those with a bent toward collecting are now "pinning" on Pinterest. The kind of people who would write numerous letters in the old days are now compulsively posting. Those who wouldn't have missed the Friday night fights are immersed in the shady world of online gambling. The sort who would be inclined to argue politics face to face in an earlier day post their grievances on social media and in comments sections today.

And then there are all the new enticements we couldn't have imagined before they showed up: video sharing, photo-manipulation apps, viral hashtags, virtual reality, and so much more.

So we go to our gadgets again and again, like an addict to heroin.

Our world has become a constant feed of information and entertainment. We take our phones with us everywhere we go. We connect to the internet wirelessly from thousands of locations. We are fed messages relentlessly from advertisements everywhere we look. And we are bombarded with a twenty-four-hour news cycle.

Each bit of information enters our minds with one goal: to gain control of our attention and resources. At the same time, it pulls our attention from the work right in front of us. Equally important, tech distractions keep us from realizing the life we truly desire to live . . . and yet these distractions go virtually unnoticed.

We never expected technology to become so pervasive in our lives. And while we appreciate the benefits, we rightly wonder what these advantages are costing us. Computer scientist Cal Newport wrote,

> These technologies as a whole have managed to expand beyond the minor roles for which we initially adopted

them. Increasingly, they dictate how we behave and how we feel, and somehow coerce us to use them more than we think is healthy, often at the expense of other activities we find more valuable. What's making us uncomfortable, in other words, is this feeling of *losing control*— a feeling that instantiates itself in a dozen different ways each day, such as when we tune out with our phone during our child's bath time, or lose our ability to enjoy a nice moment without a frantic urge to document it for a virtual audience.

It's not about usefulness, it's about autonomy.[1]

How, then, do we recognize these large—yet subtle—distractions in our lives? How do we regularly assess the path of our lives to ensure that we're seeking and investing in the most significant things? Perhaps it's not as hard as we imagine. Maybe it requires only a little intentionality and effort. And often, realizing what's going on is the first step.

## How Screen Use Distracts Us from Purpose

Our Things That Matter Survey asked, "How much does the distraction of technology (games/social media/connectedness) keep you from fulfilling your purpose in life?" A total of 57 percent of respondents answered "somewhat" or "a great deal."

The other 43 percent may not be taking into account just how much technology is intruding in their lives.

According to the Nielsen Total Audience Report of August 2020, the average time a US adult spent consuming media in that year totaled twelve hours and twenty-one minutes per day. In case you didn't notice, that's *slightly over half the number of hours in a day and about three-quarters of our waking hours.* The two largest categories were smartphones at three hours and forty-six minutes per day and television at three hours and forty-three minutes per day.[2] On average, people open their phones fifty-eight times a day (thirty of them during the workday), with most of the sessions lasting under two minutes.[3]

Does the distraction of technology (games/social media/ connectedness) keep you from fulfilling your purpose in life?

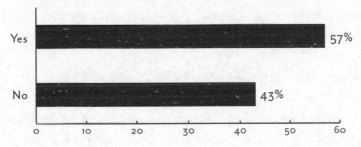

The numbers are similar in the UK, even a bit worse. Research polling found that Britons spend more than 4,866 hours a year (or more than 13 hours per day) on their gadgets. This equates to 301,733 hours—or *34 years*—over a lifetime.

How much time do *you* spend on your devices? More importantly, have you ever thought about how much of it is productive and how much of it is a detriment to productivity?

Things that matter usually take time, energy, and concentration. Is devoting our time to binge-watching movies on TV or beating the next ten levels of *Candy Crush* really worth it? It might be, if it gives us some much-needed diversion from our real-life stresses. Probably not, though, if these distractions have become a lifestyle and are taking us away from the pursuits we've identified as most meaningful to us.

And here's how it happens:

## 1. The Overuse of Technology Steals Your Time

One of the most common excuses for not pursuing one's goals in life is "I don't have time." And every one of the distractions we've looked at in this book is a time stealer. But the worst of all in this respect is technology.

If you're like many people, you're spending up to three-quarters of your waking hours interacting with technology. That probably includes the hours of the day when you are most alert and could be most productive. Cut back on your screen time, and you will have taken the single most effective step to opening up more time for more meaningful pursuits.

## 2. The Overuse of Technology Makes You Feel Bad About Yourself

This is true for much of entertainment and advertisement, but the worst offender here is social media. Along with letting you keep up with friends, it can so easily make you wish you had someone else's life.

Can we be honest? Everyone is writing fiction on social media. Nobody posts their photos of sitting on the couch eating potato chips in an empty house while watching television (unless maybe it's the new hit show). Most people post only the highlights of their lives.

So if you find yourself scrolling media constantly and experiencing discontent with your own life—wishing you had a bigger house, a more lavish vacation, a better seat at the concert, a more attractive family, or a fancier purse—you may have fallen under the spell of tech's fiction. Give it a miss, because you can create a new, more purposeful and meaningful you only if you dwell in the nonfiction of your life.

## 3. The Overuse of Technology Makes You Weaker

Our devices deliver benefits, but they also exact costs. The medical evidence is in: a large amount of screen time can restructure your brain, with effects including "gray matter shrinkage, problems with white matter's ability to communicate, a lot more cravings, and general poorer cognitive performance."[4] In fact, "the longer you spend [watching a screen], the more at risk you might be of depression."[5] Overwatching the news is associated with anxiety.[6] Other physical effects of excess screen time include eye strain, weight gain, isolation, reduced emotional responsiveness, and disrupted sleep patterns. High amounts of screen time can even increase the risk of mortality—in one study, up to 52 percent.[7]

Scary, isn't it?

But think about the other side: reducing screen time can make you healthier and more emotionally stable and give you clearer thinking. Why wouldn't you want to be at your best to pursue the goals you consider the best?

## 4. The Overuse of Technology Makes You Less Effective in Your Work

Even if we're using our devices for strictly work-related purposes while on the job, if we do it in an inefficient manner, it can come with a surprisingly high cost. One study investigating the impact of interruptions at work showed that, on average, study participants took about twenty-three minutes to get back on task after a distraction.[8] So, potentially, that email you diverted your attention to in the middle of other work could mean twenty-three minutes of time lost for pursuing something more meaningful.

And then there's the way that technology is affecting our ability to concentrate and think at length—vital skills at work and in the rest of life. Nicholas Carr, author of *The Shallows: What the Internet Is Doing to Our Brains*, said,

What we're trading away for the riches of the Net—and only a curmudgeon would refuse to see the riches—is what [media blogger Scott] Karp calls "our old linear thought process." Calm, focused, undistracted, the linear mind is being pushed aside by a new kind of mind that wants and needs to take in and dole out information in short, disjointed, often overlapping bursts—the faster, the better.[9]

Cal Newport echoed this by saying that however valuable our digital connectedness may be, we can't lose the ability to do what he calls "deep work"—the ability to focus without distraction on a cognitively demanding task.[10]

As we saw in the preceding chapter, work is closely related to our purpose and goals in life, and even if our paycheck gig isn't our dream job, it deserves our best work because it's a way we love and serve others. Reining in our unnecessary use of tech on the job is an *immediate* and *guaranteed* way to be more present at work.

Technology is the last distraction we're looking at in *Things That Matter*—the last obstacle that must be cleared away. Unlike such distractions as fear and the selfish pursuit of happiness, technology comes to us from the outside rather than arising from within. But it has a pernicious way of getting inside us and changing our minds, hearts, and wills. It's pervasive enough and influential enough that we can't afford to assume it's okay or that we can handle it. We've got to decide who's going to be the master in our lives—us or tech.

According to business writer Eric Barker, Newport "thinks the ability to stay focused will be the superpower of the 21st century."[11] Consider how unfocused technology is making you, and I think you'll begin to agree that he's not overstating.

## The Dark Side of Technology

Bonnie Dumaine is the loving mother of two teenagers and lives in Hershey, Pennsylvania, where she and her husband serve as houseparents at a local school. Describing how technology was influencing her and the people around her, she told me:

> The more I weighed technology's influence on my life, the more I began to see the harmful side. For example, I have noticed that scrolling mindlessly on social media every day negatively affects my outlook, my self-esteem, my focus, and my mood. I notice that everyone is almost exclusively posting only the positive aspects of their lives, but it is still difficult to escape feelings of jealousy, comparison, and sadness that my reality does not compete.

Between work and family, Bonnie is a busy woman. Technology is not her friend when it takes over her schedule.

She said, "The constant availability of Netflix, Hulu, and other streaming sites easily distracts me from being productive and often traps me into addictively watching several shows in a row. I procrastinate the things I really need to get done and then feel guilty. Or stay up too late and am not my best self in the morning. Even games, which seem like a fun little diversion, too often consume my time and attention more than I intend."

Bonnie has noticed that technology has also impacted her friends and family, saying,

> I see my friends trying to keep up with the latest trends that are constantly changing. My husband and I are always helping our parents learn the latest technology or

newest updates. And my kids, who haven't touched toys
for years, find their news and lifestyle trends hourly, post
and then delete due to insecurities, and fear they are
missing out if not connected to a phone for a short
amount of time. They spend less time actually being with
people, because they are 'with' their friends on a game or
app all the time.

This is a woman who is alert enough to see that she and those she
cares about most are losing control of their lives due to the appeal of
technology. I think most of us can relate readily to her reactions. It's
time to be afraid, very afraid.

## Addictive by Design

In *Digital Minimalism,* Cal Newport said, "We added new technolo-
gies to the periphery of our experience for minor reasons, then woke
one morning to discover that they had colonized the core of our daily
life. We didn't, in other words, sign up for the digital world in which
we're currently entrenched; we seem to have stumbled backward into
it."[12] Stumbling backward into it—that sounds just like how I got
involved with blogging and social media.

*Stumbling backward* sounds harmless, almost quaint. But it's not.
Our addiction to technology is big business.

Newport went on to offer an interesting qualification to what he
had just said: "It's probably more accurate to say that we were *pushed*
into it by high-end device companies and attention-economy con-
glomerates who discovered there are vast fortunes to be made in a
culture dominated by gadgets and apps."[13]

Why are we spending so much time on our devices? Because some of the smartest people in the world are working hard to make sure we do. Business journalist Lydia Belanger said,

> From push notifications and reminders to ratings and rewards programs, technology has the power to nudge you to think and act in specific ways at specific times.
> Addictive design keeps you hooked, algorithms filter the ideas and options you're exposed to and the data trail you leave behind comes back to haunt (or target) you later.[14]

Technology designers know what they're doing when they give us simple colors and lights and sounds and haptic feedback (vibrations or other movements we feel). Other techniques include personalized ads that have been real-time A/B tested over and over again, recommended videos, variable ratio schedules (random rewards, like slot machine payouts), new levels and achievements, and social reciprocity (for example, if you add someone to your LinkedIn network, you can get access to his or her connections).[15]

---

## Why are we spending so much time on our devices? Because some of the smartest people in the world are working hard to make sure we do.

---

Adam Alter, a professor of psychology and marketing at NYU, said that our absorption with technology is directly comparable to substance addictions. It's a behavioral addiction. "The age of behavioral addiction is still young," he wrote, "but early signs point to a crisis. Addictions are damaging because they crowd out other essential pursuits, from work and play to basic hygiene and social interaction."[16]

Nir Eyal wrote a book called *Hooked: How to Build Habit-Forming Products*. In other words, he wrote the textbook many companies are using to attract and hold our attention, becoming a distraction to us and a profit source for them.

He dealt the heroin.

He's also selling the methadone.

I say that because his next book is called *Indistractable: How to Control Your Attention and Choose Your Life*. It's about how to resist the habit-forming products others produce so that you can get some work done and enjoy some autonomy.

Addressing the irony produced by putting his two books side by side, Eyal wrote,

> Companies making their products more engaging isn't necessarily a problem—it's progress.
>
> But there's also a dark side. As philosopher Paul Virilio wrote, "When you invent the ship, you also invent the shipwreck." In the case of user-friendly products and services, what makes some products engaging and easy to use can also make them distracting.
>
> For many people, these distractions can get out of hand, leaving us with a feeling that our decisions are not our own. The fact is, in this day and age, if you are not equipped to manage distraction, your brain will be manipulated by time-wasting diversions.[17]

Eyal went on to point out that this digital engineering can have a dangerous effect on society at large.

Tristan Harris, a former Google design ethicist, said it this way: "A business model that is infused in the social communications infrastructure that 3 billion people live by, and are dependent on, is misaligned with the fabric of society and specifically poses a kind of existential threat to democracy and a functioning society."[18]

Technology's existential threat to society mirrors its existential threat to the kind of people we want to become. I'm concerned that when we give in to it too much, living unintentional lives distracted by our devices, we are going to get to our final days and wonder why we wasted so much time.

If technology has become tyrannical in our lives, it's in large part because experts have deliberately made it that way. But rather than blaming others (there's no opportunity for change in blame), let's take responsibility for our part in submitting to the tyranny of tech. And let's work on getting ourselves out from under the influence of all those slick gadgets with their blinking lights.

## The Insurgency Begins Here

If the tyranny of tech is distracting you from pursuing the things that are meaningful to you—or even if you're just sick and tired of being manipulated by the masters of media and entertainment—I have one word for you: *rebellion.*

Let's open our eyes to what's happening, and let's dare to control the technology in our lives instead of letting it control us. And let's do it with a larger purpose in mind: to focus more on the things that matter most. Let's proudly wear the label of *tech rebels* and take back our lives and futures.

This is not primarily about finding hacks, like turning off notifications or using an app to monitor your use of other apps—though there's a place for all that, and we'll be getting to it. More important are the strategies to overthrow the emotional and psychological influence our devices have over us.

### Rebel against the tyranny of tech.

## Do a Digital Detox

Once a year, I take an extended break from technology. When I take a tech fast, I inevitably learn I'm more addicted than I thought. But that's the nature of addiction, isn't it? We can never fully realize our level of addiction until the item is taken away. The only way to truly discover technology's controlling influence on our lives is to turn it off, walk away, and sense how strong the pull is to turn it back on. Each time I go on digital detox, it proves to be a powerful reset for me in my relationship to technology and its offerings.

---

> The only way to truly discover technology's controlling influence on our lives is to turn it off, walk away, and sense how strong the pull is to turn it back on.

---

I've never had a food sensitivity or intolerance, such as to dairy or gluten, but I've had friends with this kind of challenge. They'll often go through a "clean" period in which they don't eat the food they suspect is causing them problems—not a drop or a crumb. Then they'll slowly reintroduce the food to see how it affects them. From there, they can decide what course is best for them.

That's what I recommend to you with your personal technology. Take a break. Then slowly reintroduce it to a healthy level—and stop there.

How about starting with a twenty-nine-day digital detox? Sure, you can do it successfully for a different length of time, but I've observed that twenty-nine days seems to give most people the right amount of time for abstaining from technology and gaining a new perspective on it.

When you're doing your digital detox, make it as comprehensive as you possibly can. I realize there are exceptions. Maybe you have to use email and text for your work. Maybe you've got teens with driver's licenses and you want to keep your cell phone on when they're out of the house. But even so, during your detox, can you go totally off social media? Or turn off the television entirely? Or never play a single video game? Or let the news headlines scream their doom without paying any attention to them? (You'll be all right, trust me.)

The more you can cut out, the more effective this exercise will be. And don't give in before the twenty-nine days are up. This is rebellion we're talking about here, after all. Don't be a wimpy tech insurgent.

---

## Five Signs You Might Need a Digital Detox

1. You spend more time on your devices than you intend.

   Technology can be like quicksand—sticky and challenging to escape. Haven't we all gotten hooked after one article and stayed for another article, comment, or share? You click on an article that should take only five to ten minutes of your time, but what if you continued scrolling down your Facebook news feed afterward? Before you know it, you've spent fifteen to twenty minutes mindlessly scrolling.

   The squandering of time is a direct and obvious consequence of the built-in attraction of games, sites, and apps. You may find it easier to disrupt this habit entirely and then start again, rather than to merely try to curb it.

2. You feel guilt or dissatisfaction after spending time with your electronic devices.

When I eat a bag of chips, I immediately feel the salt on my tongue. Eventually, the saltiness dulls and oils remain. The residue clings to my fingertips. But when I overeat on these empty calories, I feel dissatisfied.

Technology use has a similar reward-regret curve. Each site and article provides a little nugget of instant gratification. Too many, and I'm inclined to regret this use of time.

If you're filled with negative emotions after spending time on tech, that's a not-so-subtle hint that you need to go on a tech break.

3. You're motivated by a fear of missing out.

FOMO is a recognized form of social anxiety that has gotten worse in our day. It's the worry that others might be having fun online while you're not there. *If I'm not watching that video or scrolling that feed, I'm going to be the loser who isn't in on the cool thing that's happening.*

The truth is, you'll *always* miss out on something. There's always more we can participate in, but time is limited and being busier is not the answer. To teach yourself this truth, do the subversive thing and deliberately miss out on communication and entertainment.

During your twenty-nine-day fast from technology, you can give the most important people a way to get through to you in an emergency. Everything else can just wait.

4. You experience urges to check and check again.

The little red symbol says you've got fifteen new emails. What if they're important? You'd better check now!

Yes, you were on Facebook just half an hour ago. But a lot has appeared on your feed in that time.

You've already scanned the headlines on your favorite news channel several times, but since the last time, a "breaking news alert" may have started scrolling in the ticker box.

Find out how much more you can get done if you stop interrupting your own concentration—and how unnecessary nearly all that information is that you were obsessively checking on.

5. You never have enough time in your day.

Once I was talking with my kids at the kitchen counter about the distraction of technology. They got out their phones and reported their screen time and most-used apps.

"Now what about you, Dad?" said Salem.

Of course, to keep it fair, I had to check too.

What I found still haunts me. I'd picked up my phone more than fifty times that day. I'd spent more than two hours on email, social media, text messaging, and web browsing. While a lot of that was for work, it was still far more than I would have guessed or could have justified.

At the end of a day, it's not uncommon to feel like you've been incredibly busy. The busyness and stress are real, but if you were to reduce tech usage, might it help you feel calmer and more available for what matters?

## Choose Contribution over Consumption

Let me give you a powerful question to help you reestablish your tech-use habits in a better way after your digital detox: *Online, am I contributing something useful to the world, or am I just consuming things others have contributed?*

Have you ever thought about how passive most of our time with technology really is? We're reading text somebody else wrote. We're watching videos somebody else captured. We're playing a game somebody else created—literally playing by his or her rules.

# *Online, am I contributing something useful to the world, or am I just consuming things others have contributed?*

Constantly consuming media without contributing much is a big part of our current predicament of being more a serf than a free agent when it comes to technology.

Again, there may be nothing wrong with catching a sports event on TV or watching funny videos with your kids. But it's *so* easily overdone. I imagine it has something to do with the fact that consuming takes less mental energy than contributing. Also, if we have stress, it can feel soothing to us, so it becomes the kind of distraction we seek.

Does that list get a little personal? It does for me. But this isn't about feeling guilty—it's about staging a revolt against the power of these activities to suck us in and eat up our time.

If you're going to be online, emphasize being creative or contributing something worthwhile.

- Write blogs that express helpful ideas.
- Share your photos or artwork in a way that doesn't intentionally foster jealousy.
- Learn something you can use.
- Teach something you're an expert in.
- Encourage a friend who is down.
- Post images or quotes that inspire others.
- Like a post (likes are free, and each one is like a little gift of affirmation).
- Send a text to someone who's lonely.
- Share an article that's insightful.

- Recommend valuable movies or books (for starters: #thingsthat matterbook).
- Establish a fundraiser for a cause.
- Communicate the needs of others, such as a neighbor who is sick and could use premade meals.
- Post pics of belongings you want to give away.

If what you make contributes to the good of others in your time online, then it is time well spent. You can even help to change the culture of the platforms you use, at least for your friends and circle of influence, by choosing to contribute positive messages—that's what I try to do. Rather than being a passive observer, create positive change.

After all, at the end of our lives, we want to be able to look back on our choices with pride. That includes the choices we made to use technology positively.

## See Tech as More of a Tool Than a Toy

There's nothing wrong with watching an episode of *The Office* in the evening . . . unless that's just when your daughter wants to tell you about her day.

No one can blame you for taking a break from your work to read a news article . . . unless you've got a deadline looming or there's a significant opportunity for impact in front of you.

Watching football on Sundays isn't immoral . . . but leaving your family three nights a week to hang with your buddies at the sports bar probably is.

Sometimes entertainment is a well-earned diversion from a focused lifestyle. Other times it's an unjustifiable escape from life.

So after choosing contribution over consumption, another principle for helping you reestablish your relationship with technology in a healthier way is to use technology less as a toy and more as a tool. In other words, do most of the reducing of your time interacting with technology in the area of entertainment, especially silly or mindless amusement.

For example . . .

- Emails and texts keeping up your relationships with distant family members: yes.
- Hours spent watching prank videos: no.
- Online research in an area where you want to enhance your professional knowledge: yes.
- Looking for opinion pieces you know will just make you mad and then flaming the authors in the comments: no.

Only you can decide how much time is reasonable to devote to valueless but diverting entertainment. Only you can decide how tech can help you become a better person and a more effective crusader for your cause. But remember this: a tech rebel gains power by spurning the trivial, the superficial, the frivolous, the hateful, the sinful, the moronic, and the petty. Don't feed the monster that is hoping to devour you.

## Use Tips and Tricks

Countless blogs and articles offer tips and tricks to corral technology. Maybe you've tried some of them with little success. The reason they didn't work in the past might be that you didn't wrestle with the deeper philosophies underlying them. I encourage you to try them again.

But first, start with the twenty-nine-day digital detox. And then wrap your mind around the potential to contribute on the internet rather than just consume and to use technology as a tool more than as a toy. Next, try adding one or two of these tips to your life to help you succeed and stay within healthy guardrails.

Some of the practical methods people have used successfully include things like:

- Make a habit of putting away your phone when you get home.
- Create tech-free zones in your house.
- Disable notifications.
- Check email only twice a day.
- Reduce the apps on the home page of your phone.
- Use an app to shut down a device after a certain period of time.
- And much more.

No single set of guidelines is going to work for everybody. And besides, as tech changes over time, so too do the techniques that rebels like us have to use to fight it.

So set rules for yourself. Be your own gatekeeper. Choose how you will use technology instead of letting the tech titans choose for you. Do more things that make you forget about checking your phone.

For more specific guidance, I recommend the books *Digital Minimalism* and *A World Without Email* by Cal Newport.

## Is Life Without Social Media Possible?

Kinsley Smith is a mother of four young children living in a small Pennsylvania town. In 2017, she did something many of us would find unimaginable: she turned off social media for good and never looked back.

Some might describe Kinsley as a classic overachiever. She graduated at the top of her class in premed and began work on a master's degree, all while serving as the executive director of a local community center. Then her first child was born, and she chose to pursue full-time motherhood rather than full-time employment. At first it was only a temporary decision. "My husband was in a stable job," she said, "so I decided that I would take a year off work and become a stay-at-home mom. At the end of that year, I became pregnant with our second and decided that being home with my children was the most important job I could do during this stage of life."

But full-time parenting is hard work and stressful, and it's not an easy transition to go from being a public overachiever with broad freedom to being a stay-at-home mom whose daily schedule is set by two little human beings who can't even talk.

When I asked her about it, Kinsley told me,

> I found myself turning to my phone more and more to break that tension—turning to social media in the hopes it would bring some calm into my life. Sometimes even sneaking away to the bathroom for a moment alone.
>
> But social media never brought the relief I desired. In fact, it made things worse. I'd hop on social media and see many of my friends from school living the life I used to think I wanted. I saw the vacations they were taking. I could feel it making me envious and grumpy.
>
> I remember one afternoon when I had put my oldest son down for a nap and began feeding my youngest. In the stillness, I picked up my phone and began scrolling. At one moment, I looked down and my baby was staring up at me. But I hadn't even noticed because I was scrolling.
>
> I knew that was not the mom I wanted to be. When my baby looked in my face, I wanted him to see my eyes looking back at him. And I didn't want my kids feeling

like they annoyed me every time they interrupted Mom
on her phone.

At first, the plan was to turn off all social media for
three months. During the initial three months, I often
found myself craving my phone. Numerous times I just
wanted to log in to see what was happening. But that was
an alarm bell to me that my relationship with social
media wasn't healthy. So I decided to extend my experiment to a year. And then permanently.

Not all digital detoxes will end in a permanent separation from
social media. But in Kinsley's case, it has been worth it:

I am so much happier and enjoy my life so much more
now. I didn't realize how loud my soul had become—how
feelings of envy and competition and inadequacy were
present in my life because of social media. Or how much
pressure I was putting on myself by trying to focus on all
the topics and issues that influencers and other people I
knew were telling me needed to be important to me.
Now I am able to better focus on what is most important
to me.

## Powering Down to Power Up

Remember, you're not just rebelling against the tyranny of technology
in your life. You're fighting for the people and causes that mean the
most to you.

While trivial distractions are not new (television has been around
for seventy years, radio for a hundred), many of the ways technology

distracts us from things that matter are new temptations we're facing. And we need to control it in our own lives, before it controls us.

One thing is for sure: the leaders of technology are not going to stop warring for our focus, our time, and our money. We must learn to fight back in a responsible way if we're going to live lives that matter.

I want to reiterate that I believe technology can be used for good. This is not a chapter about removing it entirely from our lives. As I've pointed out, in many ways, I'm doing what I do today only because of technology. And if you're reading this book because you met me through my blog, YouTube channel, or social media feeds, you are an example of how technology has played a role in my making a difference in the world.

But let's put it in perspective. When people learned how to make fire, humanity had to adjust. Here was this amazing tool with infinite possibility to light the night, warm the body, cook food, disinfect water, and forge steel. And yet it could also burn the flesh, consume crops, and destroy entire towns and forests with its power. Fire could be used as a tool to enhance and improve life. Or, left unchecked, it could destroy life.

We face a similar turning point in the world today with respect to technology. No doubt, there's going to be a period of evaluating what is healthy and worthwhile when it comes to technology, new media, and social media. And there's going to be a period of evaluating what is unhealthy and soul robbing. My assumption is that humankind will eventually learn how to use it for good, as we've done with previous societal advancements. But in the meantime, we must do what we can to use technology as a tool for meaning rather than a distraction from it.

Bring intentionality to every technological platform and interaction you encounter. Take meaningful breaks to reevaluate its role in your life to see if powering down your devices is a way to power up your purpose.

Rebel against the shadowy motivations of tech companies who profit from your attention and information. And in the end, use technology to promote things that matter rather than being distracted from them.

# PART 4

## ENDING OF THE BOOK, BEGINNING OF A MORE MEANINGFUL LIFE

# 11

## Live the Story You Want Told
### And Expect Surprises

Dig deep enough in every heart and you'll find it: a longing for meaning, a quest for purpose. As surely as a child
breathes, he will someday wonder, *What is the purpose of
my life?*
—MAX LUCADO, *ONE GOD, ONE PLAN, ONE LIFE*

Consider this last chapter to be basically me holding out my hand to
shake your hand. Congratulations! You've begun dealing with the *biggest deterrents* to achieving the *most important things* in your life. I have
a hard time thinking of anything with a bigger payoff than that. And
you know as well as I do that not everybody is willing—or at least
ready right now—to go to the effort of figuring out how to align their
lifestyle with their intentions. But *you're* doing it. For a moment, bask
in a glow of satisfaction over how far you've come.

The inward obstacles of fear, guilt, and shame . . . looking for happiness in the pursuit of selfish desires . . . the temptations of holding
on to money that others may need more than we do and of crowding
our lives with stuff that gets in the way of purposefulness . . . the way
our course can get bent by living for others' applause and by thinking
leisure is what it's all about . . . and, of course, all those slick electronic
devices we permit to intrude upon our attention all day long. These

are things whose true nature has been revealed to you—namely, as distractions that have the power to give you a life you'll regret, if you let them. But now you won't.

I'm sure you understand that finishing this book isn't the end of struggling against distraction. As we've seen, nothing but death will be the end of anyone's struggling with that. But the struggle is different when you have clear knowledge of who your adversaries are. And when you understand how they war against your purpose. And when you're equipped to root them out, shove them aside, put them on mute.

Even then, clearing away the distractions is not the ultimate point in all this. The ultimate point is to live a life of meaning and purpose. So take advantage of the way you've taken the power position over the distractions in your life. Get going on the things that matter to you.

It's going to be quite a journey. And I've got to tell you, it may not go exactly as you anticipate.

## False Summits

At 12,637 feet, Humphreys Peak is the tallest mountain in Arizona, and it seemed a good challenge for a friend and me when we wanted to take our sons on a strenuous adventure. The ten-mile trail to the summit of this isolated mountain earns a "very difficult" rating from hikers.

Once the four of us got above tree line after several hours of hiking, we followed the main ridge and after a while came to a steeper ascent where we could see the summit. I thought with relief, *Whew, just a little more hard climbing and then we'll be done, because there's the top of the peak right up there.*

But when we reached that summit, I was disappointed to see that the trail kept going. There was another summit up ahead.

*Oh, that's right,* I thought. I remembered the sign I'd seen at the trailhead that mentioned "false summits." This was what a false summit looked like. A false summit, especially on a strenuous climb, can have a significant impact on a hiker's psyche. *Now I understand why they posted signs at the bottom,* I thought to myself.

The same thing happened again, and again, and again—me thinking we had reached the top, only to realize that our true destination still lay ahead. We'd come to another false summit.

Eventually, we stood on the rounded top of Humphreys Peak and enjoyed the 360-degree view, with Flagstaff nestled in its forest to the south and multicolored desert terrain stretching northward to the Grand Canyon.

False summits on a mountain make you think you've reached the end of the trail—but no, there's still farther to go. In my case, I'll admit, every false summit we crested (even when I was expecting it) brought with it a sinking of the heart. And every false summit required me to firm up my determination and be willing to carry on, keep going, and head toward another apex.

That's the way of it, too, when we've embarked on an intentional path of devoting our lives to the service of things that matter. It's not as simple as going from here to there. Frequent switchbacks can make us wonder if we're making any progress. Pleasant overlooks provide natural places to stop and enjoy the view we have attained. Other times, we simply need to stop in our tracks and catch our breath, fuel up with the snacks we've brought, or examine the trail signs to see if we're still going in the right direction. And then there are the false summits in our arduous pursuits.

Getting people to read my *Becoming Minimalist* blog wasn't my final destination after I started living an intentional life as a minimalist. It was just the start. I had no idea what the next peak would be. After I began using social media for good, suddenly there were books I wanted to write. Then I noticed an opportunity to build a decluttering course where I could give more personal attention to people who were serious about owning fewer possessions but struggled with finding victory. Although it hadn't occurred to me earlier, eventually adding an app made sense too.

And why stick with just minimalism? Thanks to my own simple living, I had both time and money to give to addressing a whole other realm of human need besides excess ownership—hence my nonprofit organization the Hope Effect, caring for orphans in their critical early-development years. And I haven't even begun to mention the pride I feel in being an attentive and intentional father to my kids and a faithful husband to my wife.

Today, I'm doing things and making a difference in the world in ways I never foresaw or would have dreamed I was capable of a decade or two ago. I credit intentional living for my accomplishments. That has included clearing away the distractions that would have kept me rooted in place or at least slowed down my progress. Now I view the future with enthusiasm and a sense of wide-open possibility. I'm telling you, this is way more fun than buying a bigger house, driving a more luxurious car, or planning a more exotic vacation could ever be.

Now, it could be that you have a singular goal and a simple path to get there. But it's far more common, in my experience, for people to change course not once but multiple times as they see better things ahead. Beyond Mount Thing-That-Matters lies the higher Mount New-Thing-That-Matters. The journey itself exposes fresh destinations. When we remove distractions and reach a meaningful peak—an accomplishment we have aimed for—we shouldn't be surprised when there are higher reaches beyond. We won't grow weary. Our strength will increase. Because we recognize the further peaks as amazing opportunities.

Let's you and me both be adventurers, shall we? Let's gear up for a journey that goes peak by peak by peak to places we never imagined.

## Opening Your Eyes to See

You may have wondered why I (someone who was not an orphan and didn't know many orphans) got interested in orphan care and made it one of my life's purposes. Partly it was because of my wife, Kim, telling me about her experience of being orphaned as a child. Partly it was because my pastor, Joe Darago, kept referring to orphans in his teaching. I mean, to a weird extent, he kept talking about orphans. What was that about?

One day I asked Joe why the welfare of orphans was such a passionate issue for him, and he told me his story.

About twenty-five years earlier, Joe and his wife had one biological child when—one particular evening—Joe felt called to adopt a child from a foreign country. In a relatively short time, as a series of doors opened up, the couple adopted a baby girl from South Korea.

Fifteen years after adopting their Korean child, they adopted another girl, this time from a different Asian country. Her early childhood situation was far different from that of her older sister. From infancy to age eight, this younger child had lived in an orphanage where she got little personal attention and didn't receive an education because the orphanage administrators didn't think she was smart enough to learn.

Today, Joe and his wife love these two girls equally, but every day they wake up and see the difference in early treatment of children displayed before their eyes. Their daughter from Korea—adopted as a baby—is emotionally and developmentally on a par with her peers today. She's happy and flourishing. Their other adopted daughter, after several years in their home, still has little emotional attachment to them, doesn't really understand how to be part of a family, and has made minimal progress in overcoming her developmental delays. She'll never completely get past the way her mind and emotions were formed in her first few years of life, when she lacked adult affection and attention.

Did you know that there are approximately 140 million orphans worldwide, less than 1 percent of whom will be adopted in the span of a year?[1] Many of these kids grow up in orphanages. And—like the Daragos' second adopted child—many of them reach adulthood behind others of their age in almost every measure of development. Joe opened my eyes to these facts.

My conversations with him inspired me to create the Hope Effect, putting young orphans in high-quality home-like foster care instead of impersonal orphanages. And when I needed an executive for the nonprofit, I knew right where to go. Just like me before I switched to minimalism blogging, Joe loved pastoring but was willing to take a different course in life when the right opportunity opened up. Today, he brings to our organization a more intimate understanding of the kids' needs than I ever could—because he's seen the effects of both good and bad orphan care within his own home.

The things we encounter in life have a mysterious and wonderful way of redirecting us to places where we can make a difference if we are alert and responsive as new summits begin to emerge. The choices we make might not make sense to others who are viewing our lives from the outside. But *we* know it's the right thing to do.

## Cognitive Dissidence

I have certain slogans I use over and over again because there's always someone who needs to hear them. One of the most popular is this: "You don't have to live like everyone else. In fact, you'll probably be happier if you don't."

> ## "You don't have to live like everyone else. In fact, you'll probably be happier if you don't."

Think about all the distractions from part 3 of this book. Aren't those distractions just the way that most people live, and *expect* to live, because they don't know of any other way?

- Living for self—everybody's doing it.
- Scrambling for more money—everybody's doing it.
- Buying more stuff—everybody's doing it.
- Trying to get noticed—everybody's doing it.
- Living for weekends and vacations—everybody's doing it.
- Grabbing a phone to entertain oneself in a free moment—oh boy, is everybody doing it.

In the above lines, I probably should have put the word *everybody* in quotes. Because it's not really every last person who is doing these things. It's just most people. You know, *the herd.*

I know it's hard to separate from the herd. We live in a culture that begs us to conform. Through its various messages, it calls us to squeeze into its mold. It exerts pressure on our minds to believe in and buy its opinions, hopes, and aspirations, even though the pursuits that define most of our culture never fully satisfy our hearts and souls. We're not supposed to think differently about anything.

And then, through conformity to culture, we lose our uniqueness. We lose our passion. We lose our energy. We lose our opportunity to choose a different future. And because we are too busy chasing the wrong things, we sacrifice our opportunities to find something greater and more fulfilling in this life.

Meanwhile, at least for many of us (I truly believe), our hearts beg us to live differently. Our spirits call us to seek our own passions. Our souls cry out for meaning. Our insides long for us to live countercultural lives.

In the course of reading *Things That Matter,* you've already faced the greatest distractions in your life. And you've been toughened by doing so. Now it's time to face up to something else: the truth that you're inevitably going to be different from others. You're going to stand apart from the crowd.

Some may not like your originality. Some may be critical. But I think you'll find that many others will admire it. They may even be attracted to your example and inspired to follow it. That's my experience anyway. There's more dissatisfaction in the herd than we may suppose. As I said early on in this book, you can become a model to others of living an intentional life that has meaning.

So go on—be countercultural, be contrarian, be nonconformist. You don't have to shove your distinctiveness in other people's faces, but you also don't need to hide it. Embrace it.

What's the alternative? All a herd does is mill around, grazing. Who wants that?

You've got places to go, peaks to climb, and things to do. Good things.

## Leaving the World a Better Place

Years ago, fresh out of the University of Nebraska with degrees in banking and finance, I went to work as an intern at a large church in Omaha. It was a fantastic experience for a young man. I am grateful for the opportunity I was given early in my development.

At one point, during a meeting with over twenty pastors, the senior pastor made a statement I remember all these years later. In fact, I can still picture the room, the spot where I was sitting, and the spot where the senior pastor was standing when he made the statement. He said quite simply, "I try to leave every room I enter a little bit better than how I found it."

Not necessarily brand-new information about personal responsibility, but there was something in his sincerity that made the message stick. He continued on to list specific examples from his life about putting this into action: cleaning up rooms in his house, straightening up rooms in the church, even wiping down the counters in every public restroom he uses.

"My goal is to leave the room just a little bit nicer for the next person."

When he was finished, he led us outside to the parking lot, where we picked up every piece of trash we could find. Twenty men and women in office attire, walking shoulder to shoulder from one end of the parking lot to the other, picking up trash along the way. Lesson learned and, apparently, never forgotten.

The big goals we choose to pursue in life will give us a sense of fulfillment and satisfaction—of unselfish happiness. They can be as exhilarating as finally reaching a mountain summit after a long hike. But the personal benefits are by-products. The goal itself is centered on meeting others' needs.

Pursuing things that matter will make us more interesting and distinctive, compared to the indistinguishable herd. But regardless of which way your story line goes and which way mine goes, one way all of us pursuers of purpose can judge whether our actions really matter is to ask if they're being beneficial to others. Because of your intentional living . . .

- Are relationships healthier?
- Are the poor better off, or the sick healthier, or the uneducated better informed?
- Is our physical world in better shape?
- Is there more beauty to enjoy?
- Is there more wisdom to follow?
- Is there more kindness for people's fragile hearts?

Obviously, you can't address all the world's problems, but sooner or later there should be *something* tangible or identifiable to show for what you're doing. And if so, then when you come to the end of your life, you'll be able look back and honestly say that you've done something to make the world a better place than it was when you came into it. Your life mattered. There will be no regret in that.

## Unity on the Home Front

Choosing to give away more money, living with fewer possessions, or approaching time off in a different way—these kinds of things can not only surprise onlookers but also personally affect those who are closest to you. Taking on a new kind of service work that takes priority over your earlier pastimes—that, too, can affect your loved ones. And you'd better not ignore it.

A few years ago, I was talking with a woman who was going through my Uncluttered course. She and her husband were both professionals who had good-paying jobs. They had entered into marriage with a mutual understanding of how their lives together would unfold: make lots of money and live large, have one child, then retire early and pursue a carefree "good life." Her husband was still intent on living that way. The wife, however, had begun looking at things in a different way.

I thought she was going to ask me how to approach her husband about minimizing—I've gotten questions like that before. But it turns out, her interest in reducing their possessions was just the first sign of the changes she was contemplating.

"Joshua, how can I tell Preston that I want to quit my job to work for half the pay as the lawyer for a nonprofit? Although it will mean less money for us, it will mean more impact in the world. But still, it's different from what he thought I was becoming."

I don't remember exactly what I told her, although I tried my best to offer helpful advice. But since then, I've thought about this issue a lot more.

When people are making big changes in their lives that affect others, the first thing I advise is to measure how close the relationships with those others are. If your spouse or teenage child is going to be affected by these changes, that is a close relationship and so the loved one's responses are important to take into consideration. If your great-aunt doesn't get it, or a coworker thinks you're off your rocker, well, maybe that doesn't need to bother you so much.

For dealing with someone in your own home who is concerned or even upset about the changes you're contemplating, communication is everything. Tell them what you're thinking about doing and why you're motivated to do it. Ask their viewpoint, not to manipulate "buy-in" but because they will have a different viewpoint from you, as well as feelings that you genuinely need to take into consideration.

In your passion for doing things that matter, don't overlook the importance of your relationships with your partner and kids (if any). These relationships are important things that are built into your life. As I said in an earlier chapter, while plotting a future filled with more meaningful activity, it is important to remind ourselves of the value of the most important duties in front of us. Those duties include maintaining healthy relationships with the people we're committed to.

When you get to the end of your life, you won't just want to have few regrets about what you did with your life. You will also want to have few regrets about *how* you did those things.

So never let go of your love, because that's a loss, no matter how many other wins you have in life. I'll say it again: never let go of your love. Don't alienate those closest to you. Try instead to turn them into your allies, partners, and cheerleaders. Your team.

Meanwhile, it's only fair that *you* be ready to join *their* team. Encourage others you care about to avoid wasting their time on a "heedless luxury" and a "no good activity" (Seneca, remember?) and instead pursue meaningful goals and purposes. Then be their ally, their partner, their cheerleader.

In chapter 5, I told the story of taking a group of teenagers to Ecuador for a short-term mission trip that included a day with garbage-dump dwellers. It was a life-changing trip for all of us. One thing that disturbed me about that trip was what happened before we left. Several parents refused to let their teenagers go on the trip, even though the kids were eager to go.

"It's up to you, of course," I would say to the parents. "But I'm curious. Why don't you want them to go?"

The answer was always some variation of this: "Well, I'm worried it won't be safe enough for them."

I've seen it happen dozens of times. I guess there was some risk to that mission excursion, as on any international trip, but honestly, not that much. Certainly the possible dangers were nothing in comparison to the *certainty* that the young people who stayed home would miss out on an opportunity to have their eyes opened to a greater magnitude of need and to have their sensitive young hearts flooded with compassion. I hope those parents and kids don't regret it.

## Sharing the Journey

I'm afraid that I'm driven back on a cliché for my last word to you. (But then, clichés stick around in the language so long because they're so often true.) Pursuing things that matter and are meaningful to you is *more about the journey than about the destination.* There it is.

I've used words like *achievement* and *accomplishment* a lot in this book because we will reach some goals and arrive at some peaks in our journey. But it's really the lives we make along the way that are the ultimate regret-resistant products of our new pursuits.

The distractions in our lives have a way of making us hectic and unfocused, causing our days to pass like cards being shuffled while we hardly notice what distinguishes one from the other. Curiously and marvelously, a life of purpose is not only more productive but also usually more peaceful, because we know we're doing what we should be doing and we can relax. So take advantage of this new purpose in your life to maximize your relationships, celebrate the special moments, and really feel the sadness and joy and other emotions your experiences call forth.

> Take advantage of this new
> purpose in your life to
> maximize your relationships,
> celebrate the special moments,
> and really feel the sadness and joy
> and other emotions your
> experiences call forth.

And as possible, amid all this, allow others to share in your journey. When I began my *Becoming Minimalist* blog, I had no idea I would still be writing it more than a decade later. I thought it would have a brief life cycle and maybe a few people would find it interesting and share their own stories with me. Also, I wanted a means of collecting my ideas on what was to me a whole new way of thinking—minimalism. Putting words together has always been clarifying for me.

I'm so glad I've kept up with it all these years. Not just because it's the basis of my mission and my livelihood today, but because it is *still* a means of sharing with others while clarifying my own evolving thoughts—just with a higher visibility than used to be the case.

How can you share your journey with others? A blog might be the answer for you, as it was for me. But there are many other possibilities. Maybe you post progress reports for your friends on social media. Maybe you put together an informal council of advisors that you meet with over video sharing. Maybe you simply have spur-of-the-moment conversations with family and friends.

The point is, don't pursue the things that matter to you all alone in some dark cave of your own creating. Bring them out into the light of day, where you and others alike can receive encouragement for the future. Speak your meaningful pursuits out into the world.

Someday someone will ask you some form of this question: "How can I live for things that matter and escape regret?"

You'll have your answer ready: "You choose well. You set aside lesser pursuits to seek meaning in your life. And you do it every single day. Let me tell you about my story . . ."

## Your Turn

I once had a conversation with a dying man, an acquaintance of mine. I asked him what he had been doing since the last time I had visited him.

"I'm just trying to make the most of my remaining days," he said.

I thought to myself, *That's good advice. We should all be trying to make the most of our remaining days, no matter how many of them there may be.*

And now it's time for me to say goodbye as you continue on your journey of making the most of your life.

You've identified pursuits that have meaning for you. You've looked deep inside yourself at your fears and desires and begun the hard work of eliminating whatever distracts you from your purpose. I truly believe you've got things ahead of you that you can't even imagine right now—beautiful things, inspiring things, unimaginable views, and things you wouldn't want to miss for the world.

If you want to tell me the story of how you're pursuing things that matter, email me at joshua@becomingminimalist.com. I'd love the chance to read and be inspired by it.

But first I have something else I'd like you to do.

I want you to write the last sentence of this book for me, because now I'm done and you're in charge. This is your life to live well. Get out a pen or pencil, if you would, and finish this chapter:

*This is the beginning of my new commitment to pursue things that matter. Today, I will remove distractions so that I can* _____

_____ .

## Discover Your Purposes

What matters most in your life?

You may already know the answer to that question. In my experience, many people have a general sense of what matters most to them, though they could use help in clarifying those goals and being intentional in letting those goals shape their lives. Others are still trying to figure it out. If you've been searching for a purpose in life or just want to reevaluate your current thinking on the matter, this guide will give you the tools to do that. It's beneficial for us to revisit our goals from time to time as our lives, families, and passions change.

First of all, I don't think there is one "correct" answer for each person. You have a number of pursuits and passions that would lead to a fulfilling life—so take some comfort in that. It's not, however, an infinite number. And you don't have an infinite amount of time to engage in those pursuits. So it's crucial to have as clear an idea as you can of your biggest purpose so it can affect your daily and long-term choices.

Once you have an idea of a mission you can accomplish with your life, begin making moves toward it.

I once had a dream for my life and mentioned it to a man named Rudy Sheptock one afternoon while we ate lunch together at a Burger King. Rudy was highly influential in my life during college. I greatly admired him, and I wanted his opinion and advice. His words that day about my dream for my life have resonated in my heart through most of my greatest pursuits.

"Sometimes dreams are like grocery store doors," he said. "They may look closed from where you're standing, but once you begin taking steps to fulfill them, the door will open right when you're ready for it."

## The Intersection

The truth about what matters most to you is already in you. You already know what problems in the world stir you to action, what opportunities you like to seize, and where you see the best results. You probably already have a good sense of the obligations in your life. But maybe you haven't viewed those things as important hints toward your purpose. So here's a great way to access that information: find the

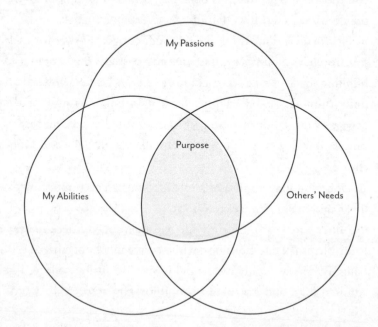

intersection of your passions, your abilities, and others' needs. Think of it as a Venn diagram where these three realities overlap.

## My Passions

Your passions are the things that get you excited. The activities that make you lose track of time, the topics you can't stop thinking about, the issues or people that touch your heart.

For example, as you know by now, I'm passionate about helping others own less so that they can live more. I've been doing it for more than a decade now, and it doesn't get old to me. I still get excited when I see people giving the gift of freedom to themselves. I get to have a little part in that—it's great! But I am also passionate about my faith and my family and developing healthy habits that contribute to an intentional life.

Others are passionate about the theater, the environment, prayer and meditation, youth sports, politics, nutrition, children's education, fitness, or their corporate mission. The options are endless, and thankfully we all have different favorites.

## My Abilities

Your abilities are your natural or acquired talents and competencies. They could be things you've always been good at, such as inspiring others in a cause or showing empathy to the hurting, or skills as specific as carpentry, cooking, and computer programming. Or they could be skills you discovered or developed later in life. They could also include knowledge, such as how to keep audit-safe books for a company, how to speak Mandarin, or how to solve problems quickly.

I have a natural ability in communicating, both through speaking and through writing. But I didn't realize I could write in a way that resonated with people until I was in my midthirties. Simply put, it was a gift, but I didn't realize it right away. When I discovered I had it, the "abilities" circle in my Venn diagram began to expand and offer a new purpose for my life.

Likewise, your abilities are gifts to you that you can give to the world.

## Others' Needs

This category may include caring for the needs of a person in your household who has a chronic illness, helping out a foster family in your community, or giving relief funds to a nation facing the aftermath of a natural disaster. It may look like seeing a need to support through an online forum for parents of children recently diagnosed with a terminal illness, or it might look like sitting and grieving with the new widow on your block. In other words, you may find that you're drawn to help others on an individual level more than a global level, or the other way around. Circumstances certainly dictate ways we can help and serve others too, so this is an important piece to revisit over time.

This is the category that begins to separate *goals* from *purpose*. Hiking the Grand Canyon may be a *goal* that drives you (and there's nothing wrong with that), but using your love for hiking to connect with a wayward son or mentor a fatherless boy may be your *purpose*.

If you're ever tempted to feel burdened by all the needs around you, remember the Venn diagram. You're not signing up to help with all the problems of the world; you're focusing on just the ones that overlap with your passions and abilities.

## Putting It Together to Find What Matters Most to *You*

All three categories in your Venn diagram are necessary for finding your life purpose.

If you're not passionate about something, it's unsustainable.

If you're not capable of doing it, it's unrealistic.

If it doesn't meet a need, it's unhelpful.

Where these three categories overlap is where you can be the most fruitful and most fulfilled.

To help you clarify your passions, your abilities, and the needs that you respond to, I'm going to invite you to ask yourself some key questions. Again, the truth about what matters most to you is already in you—as you progress through these questions, they'll help sharpen your view.

I've left space for you to write the answers. But even if you don't want to pull out a pen for that, at least stop and think for a while about each question before moving on. Your deepest insights about yourself might not come immediately.

## Identifying Your Passions

### 1. What Type of Work Excites Me?

When most of us hear the word *work,* we immediately think of the job we do to pay the bills. But for this question, think beyond your job. In the dictionary, the definition of *work* has nothing to do with a paycheck. It is simply "exertion or effort directed to produce or accomplish something."[1] That's what I mean here.

Maybe when you think about *work that excites you,* your job is the first thing that comes to mind. It is for me. That's not the case for everybody, but if your *job* and *work that excites you* are the same thing, you're one of a lucky group.

If that's not true for you, what type of *productive activity* excites you? Maybe it is gardening or painting or cooking. Maybe it is writing, leading, or building. Maybe there are some aspects of your job that you really do enjoy, even if the entire situation doesn't excite you.

As you begin to define a purpose for your life, *what work you enjoy doing* is the most important place to start. Your purpose in life won't necessarily be easy, but it is usually something you are at least drawn to.

I make my living by helping others discover the joys and benefits of minimizing. In that way, my job is work that excites me (not every aspect of it, but most). On the other hand, I make nothing from the Hope Effect, the orphanage nonprofit I started. But I still love and get excited about that work, shaping its vision, leading the board, and speaking into the culture of the organization. It's *work* that excites me, even though it's not my job.

So as you answer this question, think about what parts of your job feel most natural to you or present challenges you want to sink your teeth into. What is your dream job—and more importantly, why is that your dream job? When you're not at your job, what type of work excites you the most? If you could craft a perfect volunteer situation for yourself, what would it entail?

*Types of work that reveal where my passions lie:*

1. _____

2. _____

3. _____

## 2. What Experiences (Positive and Negative) Have Shaped My Understanding of the World and What I Care About?

We're all, at least in part, a product of our pasts. Certain experiences have effects that resound throughout the rest of our lives. Some experiences of our pasts are positive, some are negative, but they've all played a role in shaping us. For this question, list the top four or five experiences that come to mind when you consider the question *What experiences have shaped me the most?*

A child of missionaries who grew up in foreign countries feels like a citizen of the world.

A woman with a younger sister who has a developmental disability sees the world differently.

A man who grew up watching his wealthy father waste money will have certain views on wealth.

A teenager who loses his father in a car accident will have his world changed in an instant. As would a father who lost his son to a tragedy.

*The four or five experiences of my past that have most shaped who I am today:*

1. _____

2. _____

3. _____

4. _____

5. _____

## Identifying Your Abilities

### 3. What Things Do I Do Well?

What skills do people compliment you on or ask you (or pay you) to do for them? A knack for something that some people have and other folks envy.

Don't think about this one too hard; the abilities that come to mind quickly are probably the truest. They might range from the seemingly trivial (playing golf) to the obviously significant (making medical diagnoses)—and that's okay. Write down ten (or even more) of them so that you can remember them. Then, as you look them over, ask yourself, *Do any of these suggest a pattern?*

*Things I do well:*

1. _____
2. _____
3. _____
4. _____
5. _____
6. _____
7. _____
8. _____
9. _____
10. _____

## 4. What Characteristics Would I Use to Describe Myself?

Understanding your unique makeup and how it's important to the world is one of the greatest gifts you can give yourself—and others. These attributes aren't the same as your talents and skills. Here we're talking about things like your personality, temperament, values, personal style, and propensities.

You may already have taken personality tests that will help you here. Myers-Briggs? Enneagram? DISC? Knowing your attributes will help you understand which of your pursuits will fit you most comfortably. As an added bonus, self-awareness helps us become more comfortable with who we are rather than wishing we could be something we're not.

*My top five personal attributes:*

1. _____
2. _____
3. _____

4. _____

5. _____

## Identify Others' Needs That Touch You

### 5. What Needs in the World Draw My Attention?

Sadly, there is no end to the needs in the world. But I've noticed something: most people seem to be drawn to one or two needs in particular. What are the problems you see in the world that repeatedly stand out to you, even when the news isn't covering them? It could be racial injustice, foster children, mental illness, poverty, affordable housing, violence against women, spiritual needs you see in the world, or a need specific to your local community. These are the needs you already pay attention to. Again, these may be global or individual, but they always say something about where to focus your passions and abilities.

*Others' needs that I find myself especially touched by:*

1. _____
2. _____
3. _____
4. _____
5. _____

### 6. What Experiences in My Past Give Me Empathy for Others in the Same Situation?

What if the pains and sufferings in your life weren't just problems you had to endure? What if you could redeem them?

One beautiful way to draw good out of pain is to comfort others who are going through the same situation. You can support and care for them like no one else when you share your own experience, whether it's your personal recovery from PTSD, grieving the loss of a child, being laid off from a job, or navigating memories of a painful childhood.

Some of the experiences here may overlap with your answers in question 2, and that's to be expected. Likely you listed some of your greatest pains as among your most influential experiences. The difference here is that you should be specific on any pains or sufferings that have resulted in empathy for others who are in the same situation. List as many as you can.

*My own problems that have sensitized me to the problems of others:*

1. _____
2. _____
3. _____
4. _____
5. _____

## Top Three

I hope it's becoming much clearer to you what matters most to you in life. As we learn about ourselves more and more, as we stack new and different talents and life experiences into our lives—the kinds of things we've evaluated with the six questions above—we become more and more acquainted with the unique role we can fulfill in the world.

As your life situation and relationships change, the interests that congregate in the center of your Venn diagram are likely to change a bit too. But now that you're more aware of your passions, your abilities, and the areas in which you can serve others, you'll be ready to spot new opportunities when they arrive.

Take a look—either on paper or in your mind's eye—at where your passions, your abilities, and others' needs overlap.

*The top three meaningful activities that come to mind as a result of this convergence:*

1. _____

2. _____

3. _____

Stepping back, would you agree that those three things are what matter most to you right now? In other words, do the Venn diagram results resonate with you? If not, what would you change about them? I'm going to include a blank diagram on this page that you can

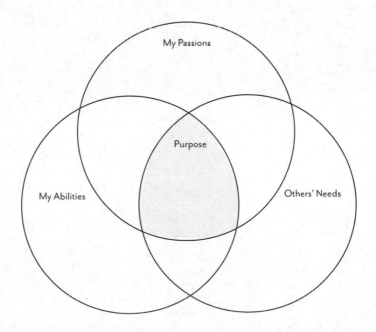

complete. Based on your answers earlier, what abilities come to mind? What passions come to mind? And what others' needs immediately come to mind?

One more thing to think about as we wrap up this exercise: If someone looked at your daily life, would he or she guess that these are the three things most important to you? Why or why not? What changes might you need to enact to make these three things remind you—and the world—that you know what matters most?

At the very least, take one step right away to move toward fulfilling your purpose. Even if you still have some uncertainty about where you should be heading, don't let that become one more distraction from making progress. Get moving! The world is full of pathways. You can take detours onto different trails whenever you need to, as long as you're moving forward to a future of no regrets.

# DISCUSSION QUESTIONS

*Things That Matter* brings to the surface a crucial truth that most of us already understand but too often ignore: Although we *want* to live lives of meaning—to do things that matter—with our limited time on this earth, the reality is that we waste a lot of our time on less important things. We let ourselves become distracted from our highest goals and our true purpose. And one great work of our lives is to overcome these distractions, freeing ourselves to live more intentionally and do the highest things of which we are capable. Understanding and agreeing with this is the easy part. The hard part is actually making the change to get there.

That's where this discussion guide comes in, because it's all about *applying* the message of *Things That Matter*.

Now, you *could* use this guide on your own, and you would no doubt get some benefit from it. But I urge you to use it with a group, because talking the issues over with others will help you process your experiences, clarify your goals, and consolidate your courage to start making changes. As a proverb puts it, "If you want to go fast, go alone, but if you want to go far, go together." A discussion group will help you go further in implementing the principles of *Things That Matter*.

This discussion guide is designed to be used in six sessions over a six-week period. To make the most of your group time, read the relevant chapters of the book prior to each session. Come to the group time with some reactions and questions in mind. Then, as you meet together, challenge one another, encourage one another, and hold one another accountable.

You'll be doing one another a huge service—helping each person leave behind a life of regrets and get on a course that leads to deep satisfaction and justifiable pride.

# WEEK 1

*Based on chapters 1 and 2*

This week's big idea: Living a life with no regrets—a life of doing things that matter—begins by removing distractions.

For most of us, it's common to have nagging anxiety that we're squandering our time and resources on things that are not important while not focusing enough on the things and people that really do matter. Something's got to change here. And there's only so much time ahead in each of our lives to make the change.

We're always going to make some foolish decisions along the way that we wish we could take back. So it's probably not possible to live a life with absolutely *no* regrets. But it most certainly *is* possible to make changes that take us off the easy path of immersing ourselves in the ordinary and the immediate and put us onto a more intentional path of living a more meaningful, satisfied life.

Presented with the choice, don't we all want a life of fewer regrets and more fulfillment? Then why aren't more of us going after our dearest goals?

In a word, because of *distractions*.

Things can go from being an occasional pastime to becoming an ingrained part of our lifestyles. This is what happens when we spend all our spare time gaming. Or we exercise so much that our working out doesn't give us energy; it uses up our energy. Or we shop for hours because we don't want to go home. Or career ambitions become workaholism. If this kind of behavior continues, then we're at risk of getting to the end of our lives and wondering, *Why did I waste this life on things that don't matter? I wish I had more time.*

When a distraction becomes a lifestyle, we lose control over the lives we are living. We lose intentionality. So let's get ready to face up to our distractions.

## Discussion Questions

1.  What regrets do you have about how you've been spending your time, money, or energy?

2.  If you were to die today, what one thing (or what few things) would you be most disappointed that you weren't able to complete?

3.  Do you agree with the philosopher Seneca's claim that "life is long if you know how to use it"? Why or why not?

4. Seneca also said, "When [life] is wasted in heedless luxury and spent on no good activity, we are forced at last by death's final constraint to realize that it has passed away before we knew it was passing." What comes to your mind when you hear the phrases "heedless luxury" and "no good activity"?

5. In chapter 1, I say, "There are people in your life whom you can serve and love better than anyone else can." Do you believe this statement to be true of yourself? If so, who are those people in your life?

6. Name something you do that you consider a legitimate diversion or recreation. Name something you do (or desire) that has become so much a part of your lifestyle that it is distracting you from more important pursuits.

7. Why did you choose to read *Things That Matter*, and what do you hope to get out of this discussion group?

# WEEK 2

*Based on chapters 3 and 4*

This week's big idea: To live a life that matters, overcome the distractions of fear and past mistakes.

In *Things That Matter*, I focus on eight distractions that commonly prevent us from pursuing important goals. In this session, you'll discuss the first two of these distractions.

## The Distraction of Fear

So many people never even take the first step toward what they consider meaningful in life because they think it will be too difficult to accomplish. Or they make only half-hearted attempts that are doomed to fail, which amounts to not trying. Something is preventing them from going for it, and it's usually some form of fear.

The most common type is fear of failure. But a lot of other fears can come into play, such as fear of rejection, fear of the unknown, fear of inadequacy, fear of losing what you have—and many more.

Yet for every distraction, there is a way to pivot toward a life of greater meaning. In this case the pivot is to replace a lesser fear with a greater one—namely, the fear that you will waste your life.

It *is* possible to move beyond the fears that are holding you back, if you keep in mind what is at stake.

## The Distraction of Past Mistakes

By "past mistakes," I'm talking about anything negative you've done or that has been done to you that is preventing you from making progress or achieving accomplishments. The mistakes that may derail a person's life include dropping out of school, a foolish business venture, going bankrupt, and unfaithfulness in marriage. Then there is the harm done to you by nature or by other people, such as a disability, abandonment or neglect, chronic illness, and verbal, sexual, or physical abuse.

As I mention in chapter 4, sometimes "mistakes" isn't a strong enough word, as in cases of child abuse. Sometimes the actions in question are downright evil. Regardless, big or little, committed by us or by someone else, past mistakes have a hobbling effect on many of us.

The pivot here? Move past the past.

No, you can't change the past—but you can loosen the grip it has on you. And maybe the pain from your past will even make you better at doing meaningful things than you ever could have been without it.

No one is so guilty or damaged that they can't make something different of their future and do something meaningful in the world.

## Discussion Questions

1. Take a look at the "Five Signs the Fear of Failure Is Keeping You from Your Best Life" list in chapter 3. Give an example of how one of them is holding you back from fulfilling your greatest potential.

2. Anthropologist Ernest Becker said, "What man really fears is not so much extinction, but extinction *with insignificance.*" What have you seen in others, or felt within yourself, that would validate Becker's claim?

3. Still looking at that quote in question 2, how do you think significance might look different from person to person, based on their talents, personality, or passions in life?

4. Looking back at your answer to question 1, what steps can you take this week toward a more meaningful life *despite your fears*?

5. If you can, share with the group your answer to one of these questions:
   • What is a mistake you've made that is hindering you from pursuing your goals?
   • What is some harm that was done to you that is hindering you from pursuing your goals?

6. What past mistake (whether your own doing or something committed against you) have you already overcome in order to reach your fullest potential? What steps did you take to confront and overcome it?

7. How might your experience of a past mistake actually *equip* you to do something important?

8. Looking back at your answer to question 5, what steps can you take this week to begin confronting this past mistake?

## WEEK 3

*Based on chapter 5*

This week's big idea: To live a life that matters, overcome the distraction of the selfish pursuit of happiness.

Happiness, of course, isn't inherently a bad thing. But when we try to satisfy our desire for happiness in the pursuit of self, we fall short of the truest, most lasting forms of happiness. The pursuit of selfish desires may offer some pleasure in the short run, but in the long term, the happiness is never lasting. Misplaced, the pursuit of happiness can become the distraction that keeps us from more meaningful pursuits.

The best, most direct pathway to lasting happiness and fulfillment is to look not only at our own interests but also at the interests of others. When we begin living our lives for the sake of others, our lives immediately take on greater value. We no longer live for the benefit of one or a few; we begin living for the benefit of many.

What I've found most effective at reorienting people's focus from their own desires to others' needs is service. That is, instead of serving *ourselves,* we serve *others.* This is how we pivot away from the selfish pursuit of happiness.

When we shift our focus off ourselves, we live lives of greater meaning and greater contribution. When we serve others without concern over what we might receive in return, we experience the beauty of selfless love. And when we direct our time and money toward others, we begin to discover pursuits more valuable than material possessions, fame, beauty, or sex.

## Discussion Questions

1. Think of a time when you did something to make yourself happy but it left you with a hollow feeling because you were being selfish? How did that experience affect your view of happiness?

2. Happiness is having quite a moment in our culture today. Do you believe the pursuit of happiness can distract you from going after more meaningful goals? If so, how?

3. Share with the group your most memorable or most recent act of service. What memories do you carry with you from that experience?

4. What are some things you are currently doing to selflessly serve others? How does serving make you feel?

5. How do you think reorienting your life around service, rather than your own happiness, would change your character? Your personality? Your outlook on the future?

6. How might living a selfless life lead to fewer regrets?

7. What is one step you can take this week toward becoming more of a servant to others?

8. As a bonus exercise, what service project could your group do together? Is that something you would be interested in doing? Why or why not?

## WEEK 4

*Based on chapters 6 and 7*

This week's big idea: To live a life that matters, overcome the distractions of money and possessions.

The topics of chapters 6 and 7—money and possessions—are closely intertwined, and both present challenges we face every day.

## The Distraction of Money

Money isn't evil in and of itself. Money is amoral or neutral in itself—technically, it's just a means to facilitate the exchange of goods and services.

The question is, Is our pursuit of money distracting us from more meaningful things? Are we wasting too much of our life—desiring money and always striving to get more of it? Because when we do, we will inevitably be distracted from things that matter in the long run. When is enough enough?

In money choices, let's err on the side of generosity. In the end, we'll be prouder of the money we gave to others than the money we kept for ourselves. So the pivot here is that if we're not giving money away, we should start, and if we are giving, we should give more.

The more we remove ourselves from the self-centered pursuit of money, the more we are drawn to others-centered living. And the more we are drawn to helping others, the greater lives of lasting significance we end up living.

## The Distraction of Possessions

Except in the case of misers, the reason we pursue money so hard is usually that we want to buy more and more stuff for ourselves. Some even buy things for themselves with money they don't have. This just seems natural to us, because we live in a society that champions the pursuit and accumulation of material possessions— "the more, the better" is the mantra we are raised to believe. Yet one of our greatest distractions from pursuing our goals is our hoard of material goods.

Who can go gung ho after a challenging goal if they're constantly buying and taking care of a bunch of stuff? Who can invest in things that matter when they're too busy organizing the garage? We're drowning in possessions, and all too often our dreams are drowning with us.

When our possessions are distracting us by stealing our money, taking up our time, or obscuring our focus, the answer is to get rid of everything we don't need and then get on with our lives at a higher level of productivity. Minimizing takes effort, but on the other side of that effort is the ongoing payoff of greater freedom to accomplish the things we want.

The pivot for possessions, then, is to first own less, then want less. In other words, once you get rid of excess possessions, you'll *know* how little you need to live happily and productively, and then the desire for buying and owning will naturally fade. Contentment will free you to accumulate a record of worthwhile accomplishments instead of a houseful of material goods.

## Discussion Questions

1.  Let's talk about possessions first. Are you a minimalist?
    *   If so, describe what the minimalist journey has been like for you, especially the benefits you've found.
    *   If not, how open are you to the idea of becoming a minimalist, and why?

2. In chapter 7, I suggest that the question we should ask ourselves about any possession is "Does it promote purpose?" Name something in your home that promotes your purpose, either directly or indirectly. Name something in your home that doesn't promote your purpose (or maybe even detracts from that purpose).

3. In what practical ways does the pursuit of possessions distract us from things that matter?

4. In what area of your home can you begin the process of decluttering possessions you don't need?

5. Complete this statement: "One clear way that money is distracting me from my highest goals is . . ."

6. As I say in the overview, in the end, we'll be prouder of the money we gave to others than the money we kept for ourselves. Do you agree? If so, what does that say about how to live a life with fewer regrets?

7. What can you do to become more financially generous? For example, can you automate donations to a charity each month or reduce your eating out to once a month so that you can give away the money you save? What problems in the world would you like to help solve with your money?

## WEEK 5

*Based on chapters 8 and 9*

This week's big idea: To live a life that matters, overcome the distractions of applause and leisure.

This week we'll look at two more things that seem to be good but often are enemies of purposeful living.

### The Distraction of Applause

Finding our self-worth in recognition and approval from others is always a foolish pursuit. It negatively impacts the decisions we make and the lives we choose to live. Furthermore, applause never fully satisfies our hearts or souls. Even those who have reached the pinnacle of fame and prestige in our society long for more of the same.

Our goal should not be to secure approval from others. That is empty and fleeting. Our goal should be to live the one life we've been given to its greatest potential—whether anybody praises us for it or not.

So what's the pivot this time? Let yourself be smaller and others bigger. In other words, don't worry so much about the extent of your own reputation. Build up the reputations of other worthy people.

Never lose sight of your mission, no matter how much or how little limelight is shining on you.

## The Distraction of Leisure

I believe that for just about everybody, the most fulfilling thing we can do, in the long term, is to focus on meaningful work. By "work," I'm not just referring to a nine-to-five job. It could be parenting. Or serving on a board. Or volunteering. Many possible things. Anything that contributes good to others is *work,* regardless of whether we're getting paid for it.

And what distracts us most from that kind of work? One of the biggest things is work's opposite: leisure. Or better put, modern society's infatuation with leisure.

I'm *not* against rest, relaxation, and fun. I just don't want you to miss out on the things that matter to you because you've unthinkingly bought into our cultural notions of leisure. What I'm against is making leisure your *objective.* Because if leisure is your objective, it will inevitably displace your higher priorities.

Please don't view your work as something only to be endured or escaped. Instead, rethink your work. Regain focus and motivation to use your passions and abilities to contribute good to a society in need of them. Your work is a way of showing love to others.

This is the pivot. You do what you do well, whether you are paid or not, so that someone else can go do what they do well, and everyone benefits. That's why I call work *love*.

## Discussion Questions

1. How important is the praise of others to you? Consider the praise or recognition you'd like to hear from any source: your spouse, your family, your community, your work, your church, or the public.

2. What are the benefits of humbly sharing attention with others?

3. Describe a way in which you could begin to seek influence more than applause.

4.  What is one thing you can do this week to benefit others without being noticed or thanked?

5.  Which of the following statements would you say more accurately reflects your attitude?
    - I live for weekends and vacations. Work is just the thing I have to slog through in order to get to my time off.
    - I like weekends and vacations and how they refresh me, but I'm excited to get back to work afterward.

6.  If you're going to be a "things that matter" person, how do you need to think differently about the way you're going to spend the traditional retirement years of sixty-five and beyond?

7.  What's the connection between your work and your life purpose? Would you ever consider changing your work in some way to align the two more closely? Why or why not? (Please note: This isn't essential for pursuing things that matter. It's just a discussion question in case the book prompted the thought.)

8. What is one thing you can do at work (or home) this week as a genuine act of selflessness, not because of the recognition you will receive?

## WEEK 6

*Based on chapters 10 and 11*

This week's big idea: To live a life that matters, overcome the distraction of technology. Then go on to live a big life!

In the preceding weeks, we looked at seven distractions. I call the distractions of fear and past mistakes "distractions of a paralyzed will" because they hold us back from moving toward our goals. I call the distractions of self-centered happiness, money, possessions, applause, and leisure "distractions of the lesser good" because they make us settle for less than living a life of real impact.

We've got one more distraction left to address, and it's a universal and obvious one in this day: *the distraction of technology.*

Think about it this way: Things that matter usually take time, energy, and concentration. So is devoting our time to binge-watching shows on TV or beating the next ten levels of *Candy Crush* really worth it? It might be, if it gives us some much-needed diversion from our real-life stresses. Probably not, though, if these distractions have become a lifestyle and are taking us away from the pursuits we've identified as most meaningful to us.

Technology has a pernicious way of getting inside us and changing our minds, hearts, and wills. It's pervasive enough and influential enough that we can't afford to assume it's okay or that we can handle it. We've got to decide who's going to be the master in our lives—us or tech.

Let's dare to control the technology in our lives instead of letting it control us. And let's do it with a larger purpose in mind: to focus more on the things that matter most. Let's pivot toward purpose by becoming tech rebels, taking back our lives and futures.

Bring intentionality to every technological platform and interaction you encounter. Take meaningful breaks to reevaluate its role in your life to see if powering down your devices is a way to power up your purpose. Remember, you're a changed person now.

Over the last five weeks, you've identified pursuits that have meaning for you. You've looked deep inside yourself at your fears and desires and begun the hard work of eliminating whatever distracts you from your purpose. I truly believe you've got things ahead of you that you can't even imagine right now: beautiful things, inspiring things—things you wouldn't want to miss for the world.

## Discussion Questions

1.  Describe the role of technology in your life. For example, do you work on a computer? How much TV do you watch? Are you one of those people who reflexively pick up their phone if they have a minute of downtime?

2. How does technology help you live a life of impact? How does it hinder you?

3. On a scale from 1 to 10, how much is technology distracting you from things that matter?

4. What is one step you can take this week to get better control of technology in your daily life?

5. Since beginning this six-week study, what have you learned about your highest purposes and goals?

6. If someone looked at your daily life, would they guess what is important to you? Why or why not?

7.  Share with the group how you completed the prompt at the end of chapter 11: *This is the beginning of my new commitment to pursue things that matter. Today, I will remove distractions so that I can* _____. What is one way this group can encourage you and hold you accountable to achieve your goal?

## ACKNOWLEDGMENTS

It is a fascinating journey to review your life to determine why you view the world in the way that you do, and the writing of this book forced me to do that. Of course, it is an enjoyable journey if you are happy with how you view the world. And for me, that is entirely the case.

I dedicated this book to my grandfather Rev. Harold E. Salem, who passed away during the writing of it. The lessons about life I learned from him can be seen from the first page to the last. But he is not the only voice that has shaped my worldview.

All four of my grandparents lived lives of faith, meaning, and purpose. Arnold, Edna, Harold, and Beulah, thank you for your love and for setting an example worth following.

To my parents, Roy and Patty, your faithfulness, godliness, love, and stability have allowed me to become the man that I am. Thank you.

To my wife, Kimberly, your love and sacrifice and selflessness are on display every day of my life and on every page of this book.

To my beautiful children, Salem and Alexa, thank you for the joy you bring into my life, for helping me see the world anew, and for allowing me the opportunity to write this book.

The voices that have shaped this book do not end with my family, for I have been blessed with valuable friendships, both short-term and lifelong. Robert Thune Sr., Mark Arant, Jack and Linda Arant, Rudy Sheptock, Joe Darago, Jack and Diana Stimmel, Scott and Diane Slocum, Gregg Walsh, Jeff Kolok—you are each a part of this book. Thank you for showing me a life focused on things that matter.

Eric Stanford, this book exists only because of your brilliant talent. Thank you for pushing me repeatedly in the writing of it and your patience and faithfulness in putting my thoughts into words.

I am thankful to the entire team at WaterBrook, from cover design and illustration to editing and publicity. A special heartfelt thank-you to Susan Tjaden, who shaped the contents of this book from the very beginning.

To my agent, Christopher Ferebee, your belief in me and this book has resulted in what you are holding now.

And to the entire Becoming Minimalist community, your encouragement and support have allowed me to do what I do. Thank you.

I have, unfortunately, missed more names than I have mentioned. But I can't possibly end a list of acknowledgments without thanking Jesus, whose saving grace has allowed me and enabled me to accomplish anything resembling good with my life. Thank you.

# NOTES

## Chapter 1: A Life with No Regrets

1. Bronnie Ware, "Regrets of the Dying," https://bronnieware.com/blog /regrets-of-the-dying. See also Bronnie Ware, *The Top Five Regrets of the Dying: A Life Transformed by the Dearly Departing* (Carlsbad, CA: Hay House, 2012). The five regrets are as follows: (1) "I wish I'd had the courage to live a life true to myself, not the life others expected of me." (2) "I wish I hadn't worked so hard." (3) "I wish I'd had the courage to express my feelings." (4) "I wish I had stayed in touch with my friends." (5) "I wish that I had let myself be happier."
2. The Things That Matter Survey was conducted by American Directions Research Group on behalf of Becoming Minimalist LLC. The nationally representative survey of four hundred respondents was conducted online during February 2021. Participants were aged eighteen and older and came from the United States. Response percentages may not add up to 100 percent due to rounding. Some survey questions presented in this book have been slightly modified to allow for responses to be combined into fewer categories. Complete survey results can be seen at www.becoming minimalist.com/things-that-matter-survey.
3. Seneca, "On the Shortness of Life," in *Dialogues and Letters,* trans. C. D. N. Costa (New York: Penguin, 1997), 57.
4. For the story of my introduction to minimalism, see *The More of Less: Finding the Life You Want Under Everything You Own* (Colorado Springs, CO: WaterBrook, 2016), chapter 1.

## Chapter 2: Distracted from Meaning

1. Seneca, *Selected Letters,* trans. Elaine Fantham (New York: Oxford University Press, 2010), 115.

2. N. S. Gill, "Profile of Demosthenes," ThoughtCo., June 3, 2019, www
.thoughtco.com/demosthenes-greek-orator-118793.
3. Frank Furedi, "The Ages of Distraction," Aeon, April 1, 2016, https://aeon
.co/essays/busy-and-distracted-everybody-has-been-since-at-least-1710.
4. Olivia Solon, "Under Pressure, Silicon Valley Workers Turn to LSD
Microdosing," *Wired*, August 24, 2016, www.wired.co.uk/article/lsd
-microdosing-drugs-silicon-valley.
5. Blaise Pascal, *Pensées*, trans. A. J. Krailsheimer (New York: Penguin,
1995), 120.
6. The original source of the quote is unknown, although the earliest known
use appears to be Ernest T. Campbell, "Give Ye Them to Eat" (sermon,
Riverside Church, New York, January 25, 1970). See https://archive.org
/details/sermongiveyethem00camp/page/8/mode/2up?view=theater.

## Chapter 3: Dreams Overshadowed

1. "What Scares Us Most: Spiders or Failing? Linkagoal's Fear Factor Index
Clears the Cobwebs," Linkagoal, October 12, 2015, https://blog.linkagoal
.com/2015/10/research-reveals-fear-of-failure-has-us-all-shaking-in-our
-boots-this-halloween-1-in-3-admit-they-are-terrified-of-failure.
2. "What Scares Us Most: Spiders or Failing?"
3. Anjelica Oswald, "J.K. Rowling Shares Photos of Her Rejection Letters
for 'Inspiration,'" Insider, March 25, 2016, www.businessinsider.com/jk
-rowling-rejection-letters-2016-3.
4. "Michael Jordan 'Failure' Commercial HD 1080p," YouTube video,
posted by "Scott Cole," December 8, 2012, www.youtube.com/watch?v
=JA7G7AV-LT8.
5. "Ranking the Top 74 NBA Players of All Time," ESPN, May 13, 2020,
www.espn.com/nba/story/_/id/29105801/ranking-top-74-nba-players
-all-nos-10-1.
6. Theo Tsaousides, "Why Fear of Failure Can Keep You Stuck," *Psychology
Today*, December 27, 2017, www.psychologytoday.com/us/blog/smashing
-the-brainblocks/201712/why-fear-failure-can-keep-you-stuck.
7. Don Joseph Goewey, "85 Percent of What We Worry About Never Happens," *Huffington Post*, August 25, 2015, www.huffpost.com/entry/85-of
-what-we-worry-about_b_8028368; and Seth J. Gillihan, "How Often
Do Your Worries Actually Come True?," *Psychology Today*, July 19, 2019,
www.psychologytoday.com/us/blog/think-act-be/201907/how-often-do
-your-worries-actually-come-true.

8. Noam Shpancer, "Overcoming Fear: The Only Way Out Is Through," *Psychology Today,* September 20, 2010, www.psychologytoday.com/us /blog/insight-therapy/201009/overcoming-fear-the-only-way-out-is -through.

9. Ernest Becker, *Escape from Evil* (New York: Free Press, 1975), 4.

10. Melanie J. Kirk, "My Greatest Fear in Life," *The Post-Grad Survival Guide,* February 4, 2019, www.medium.com/the-post-grad-survival-guide /my-greatest-fear-in-life-eb425d1ec0d1.

11. L. Frank Baum, *The Wonderful Wizard of Oz* (1900; repr., Orinda, CA: Sea Wolf Press, 2019), 138.

## Chapter 4: Wounded

1. Deanna Hutchison, "How I Learned to Declutter My Mind," *Becoming Minimalist,* February 18, 2020, www.becomingminimalist.com/declutter -my-mind.

2. Meg Jay, "The Secrets of Resilience," *Wall Street Journal,* November 10, 2017, www.wsj.com/articles/the-secrets-of-resilience-1510329202.

3. Jay, "The Secrets of Resilience."

4. Jay, "The Secrets of Resilience."

5. Christine Wilkens, phone conversation with author, April 2, 2021.

## Chapter 5: The Me Monster

1. Viktor Frankl, "Preface to the 1992 Edition," *Man's Search for Meaning* (1946; repr., Boston: Beacon Press, 2006), xiv–xv.

2. Raj Raghunathan, "Why Rich People Aren't as Happy as They Could Be," *Harvard Business Review,* June 8, 2016, https://hbr.org/2016/06/why -rich-people-arent-as-happy-as-they-could-be.

3. Summer Allen, *The Science of Generosity* (Berkeley, CA: Greater Good Science Center, May 2018), https://ggsc.berkeley.edu/images/uploads /GGSC-JTF_White_Paper-Generosity-FINAL.pdf?_ga=2.11753270 .38977004.1608835647-161681/560.1608835647; Matthew Solan, "The Secret to Happiness? Here's Some Advice from the Longest-Running Study on Happiness," *Harvard Health Blog,* October 5, 2017, www. health.harvard.edu/blog/the-secret-to-happiness-heres-some-advice-from -the-longest-running-study-on-happiness-2017100512543; and Robert

Waldinger, "Learning to Take Care of Our Relationships," *Simplify*, June 1, 2017, https://simplifymagazine.com/essay/relationships.

4. Kathleen Doheny, "Looks, Money, Fame Don't Bring Happiness," ABC News, May 22, 2009, https://abcnews.go.com/Health/Healthday/story?id=7658253&page=1.

5. Heather Horn, "Promiscuity Doesn't Make People Happier," *The Atlantic*, August 22, 2010, www.theatlantic.com/national/archive/2010/08/promiscuity-doesn-t-make-people-happier/340249.

6. Compare Olga Khazan, "Fewer Sex Partners Means a Happier Marriage," *The Atlantic*, October 22, 2018, www.theatlantic.com/health/archive/2018/10/sexual-partners-and-marital-happiness/573493.

7. Temma Ehrenfeld, "Will Plastic Surgery Make You Feel Better?," *Psychology Today*, July 15, 2015, www.psychologytoday.com/us/blog/open-gently/201507/will-plastic-surgery-make-you-feel-better.

8. Emily Esfahani Smith, "You'll Never Be Famous—and That's O.K.," *New York Times*, September 4, 2017, www.nytimes.com/2017/09/04/opinion/middlemarch-college-fame.html. See also Eva H. Teltzer et al., "Mexican American Adolescents' Family Obligation Values and Behaviors: Links to Internalizing Symptoms Across Time and Context," *Developmental Psychology* 51, no. 1 (2015): 75–86, https://doi.org/10.1037/a0038434; and Veronica Huta and Richard M. Ryan, "Pursuing Pleasure or Virtue: The Differential and Overlapping Well-Being Benefits of Hedonic and Eudaimonic Motives," *Journal of Happiness Studies* 11, no. 6 (December 2010): 735–62, https://doi.org/10.1007/s10902-009-9171-4.

9. Smith, "You'll Never Be Famous."

10. P. J. O'Rourke, *All the Trouble in the World: The Lighter Side of Overpopulation, Famine, Ecological Disaster, Ethnic Hatred, Plague, and Poverty* (New York: Atlantic Monthly Press, 1994), 9.

11. Bruce P. Doré et al., "Helping Others Regulate Emotion Predicts Increased Regulation of One's Own Emotions and Decreased Symptoms of Depression," *Personality and Social Psychology Bulletin* 43, no. 5 (May 2017): 729–39, https://doi.org/10.1177/0146167217695558.

12. Marianna Pogosyan, "In Helping Others, You Help Yourself," *Psychology Today*, May 30, 2018, www.psychologytoday.com/us/blog/between-cultures/201805/in-helping-others-you-help-yourself.

13. Stephanie Booth, "How Helping People Affects Your Brain," Healthline, December 15, 2018, www.healthline.com/health-news/how-helping-people-affects-your-brain#How-your-brain-lights-up-when-you-help. See also Tristen K. Inagaki and Lauren P. Ross, "Neural Correlates of Giving Social Support: Differences Between Giving Targeted Versus Untargeted Sup-

port," *Psychosomatic Medicine* 80, no. 8 (October 2018): 724–32, https://doi.org/10.1097/PSY.0000000000000623.

## Chapter 6: Enough Is Enough

1. 1 Timothy 6:10.
2. Catey Hill, "This Is the No. 1 Reason Americans Are So Stressed Out," MarketWatch, December 17, 2018, www.marketwatch.com/story/one-big-reason-americans-are-so-stressed-and-unhealthy-2018-10-11.
3. "Majority of Investors with $1 Million or More in Assets Do Not Consider Themselves Wealthy, According to Ameriprise Study," Ameriprise Financial Services, July 17, 2019, https://newsroom.ameriprise.com/news/majority-investors-with-1-million-or-more-in-assets-do-not-consider-themselves-wealthy-according-to-ameriprise-study.htm.
4. Graeme Wood, "Secret Fears of the Super-Rich," *The Atlantic*, April 2011, www.theatlantic.com/magazine/archive/2011/04/secret-fears-of-the-super-rich/308419.
5. Jay Harrington, "Why Men Need Minimalism," *Becoming Minimalist*, www.becomingminimalist.com/why-men-need-minimalism.
6. Jay Harrington, "Ambitious Minimalism: How Owning Less Frees Us to Achieve More," *Becoming Minimalist*, www.becomingminimalist.com/ambitious-minimalism.
7. R. Andres Castaneda Aguilar et al., "September 2020 Global Poverty Update from the World Bank: New Annual Poverty Estimates Using Revised 2011 PPPs," *World Bank Blogs*, October 7, 2020, https://blogs.worldbank.org/opendata/september-2020-global-poverty-update-world-bank-new-annual-poverty-estimates-using-revised.
8. To find out how rich you are from a global perspective, go to Giving What We Can, www.givingwhatwecan.org/how-rich-am-i.
9. Wood, "Secret Fears of the Super-Rich."
10. Benjamin Preston, "The Rich Drive Differently, a Study Suggests," *New York Times*, August 12, 2013, https://wheels.blogs.nytimes.com/2013/08/12/the-rich-drive-differently-a-study-suggests. In case you're interested, BMW drivers are the worst offenders.
11. Benjamin Franklin, quoted in S. Austin Allibone, comp., *Prose Quotations from Socrates to Macaulay* (Philadelphia: J. B. Lippincott & Co., 1876), 128.
12. Howard R. Gold, "Price Tag for the American Dream: $130K a Year," *USA*

*Today*, July 4, 2014, www.usatoday.com/story/money/personalfinance /2014/07/04/american-dream/11122015.

13. Greg McBride, quoted in Anna Bahney, "Nearly a Quarter of Americans Have No Emergency Savings," CNN, June 20, 2018, https://money.cnn .com/2018/06/20/pf/no-emergency-savings/index.html.

14. "World Hunger Is Still Not Going Down After Three Years and Obesity Is Still Growing—UN Report," World Health Organization, July 15, 2019, www.who.int/news/item/15-07-2019-world-hunger-is-still-not -going-down-after-three-years-and-obesity-is-still-growing-un-report; and WWAP (United Nations World Water Assessment Programme), *United Nations World Water and Development Report 2014: Water and Energy*, 2014, https://unesdoc.unesco.org/ark:/48223/pf0000225741, 2.

15. "401(k) Participants' Investing Behavior May Leave Them Short," Charles Schwab, www.aboutschwab.com/schwab-401k-participant-study-2019.

16. Nicole Lyn Pesce, "A Shocking Number of Americans Are Living Paycheck to Paycheck," MarketWatch, January 11, 2020, www.marketwatch .com/story/a-shocking-number-of-americans-are-living-paycheck-to -paycheck-2020-01-07; and Amanda Dixon, "A Growing Percentage of Americans Have No Emergency Savings Whatsoever," Bankrate, July 1, 2019, www.bankrate.com/banking/savings/financial-security-june-2019.

17. Lara B. Aknin et al., "Prosocial Spending and Well-Being: Cross-Cultural Evidence for a Psychological Universal," *Journal of Personality and Social Psychology* 104, no. 4 (2013): 635–52, https://doi.org/10.1037/a0031578.

18. Elizabeth W. Dunn, Lara B. Aknin, and Michael I. Norton, "Prosocial Spending and Happiness: Using Money to Benefit Others Pays Off," abstract, *Current Directions in Psychological Science* 23, no. 1 (February 2014): 41–47, https://doi.org/10.1177/0963721413512503.

## Chapter 7: Litter on the Road to Purpose

1. Ernest Becker, *Escape from Evil* (New York: Free Press, 1975), 4–5.

2. Becker, *Escape from Evil*, 84–85.

3. Jessica Pishko, *In the Red* (Seattle: Little A, 2016), Kindle.

4. Pishko, *In the Red*.

5. "Prior to the 40-year period 1977–2017, total giving was consistently at or above 2.0% of GDP. It fell below 2.0% throughout most of the 1970s, 1980s, and 1990s. Total giving as a percentage of GDP rose to 2.0% and above through most of the 2000s, but then dropped to 1.9% in the years 2009 to 2011. Total giving as a percentage of GDP was 2.1% for four of

the five years, 2013–2017." "Giving Statistics," Charity Navigator, www
.charitynavigator.org/index.cfm?bay=content.view&cpid=42.

6. "GDP (Current US$)—United States," World Bank, https://data.worldbank
.org/indicator/NY.GDP.MKTP.CD?locations=US.

7. Maurie Backman, "You Don't Need That: Average American Spends Almost $18,000 a Year on Nonessentials," USA Today, May 7, 2019, www
.usatoday.com/story/money/2019/05/07/americans-spend-thousands-on
-nonessentials/3945020 7.

8. John Ruskin, Notes by Mr. Ruskin on Samuel Prout and William Hunt
(London: Strangewater & Sons, 1879–80), 96.

9. "Average Minutes Per Day Men and Women Spent in Household Activities" (2015), American Time Use Survey, US Bureau of Labor Statistics,
www.bls.gov/tus/charts/household.htm.

10. Linda Gorman, "Hours Spent in Homemaking Have Changed Little
This Century," The Digest, National Bureau of Economic Research, October 2008, www.nber.org/digest/oct08/hours-spent-homemaking-have
-changed-little-century.

11. Amy Morin, "7 Scientifically Proven Benefits of Gratitude," Psychology
Today, April 3, 2015, www.psychologytoday.com/us/blog/what-mentally
-strong-people-dont-do/201504/7-scientifically-proven-benefits-gratitude.

12. Mary MacVean, "For Many People, Gathering Possessions Is Just the
Stuff of Life," Los Angeles Times, March 21, 2014, www.latimes.com
/health/la-xpm-2014-mar-21-la-he-keeping-stuff-20140322-story.html.

13. Alain de Botton, Status Anxiety (New York: Vintage, 2005), 43.

## Chapter 8: Trending

1. Scott Barry Kaufman, "Why Do You Want to Be Famous?," Scientific
American, September 4, 2013, https://blogs.scientificamerican.com/beautiful
-minds/why-do-you-want-to-be-famous.

2. Orville Gilbert Brim, Look at Me! The Fame Motive from Childhood to
Death (Ann Arbor: University of Michigan Press, 2010), 28.

3. Kaufman, "Why Do You Want to Be Famous?"

4. Benedict Carey, "The Fame Motive," New York Times, August 22, 2006,
www.nytimes.com/2006/08/22/health/psychology/22fame.html.

5. Rebecca J. Rosen, "Something Like 0.0086% of the World Is Famous,"
The Atlantic, January 22, 2013, www.theatlantic.com/technology
/archive/2013/01/something-like-00086-of-the-world-is-famous/267397.

6. Oluebube Princess Egbuna, "Distracted by Fame?," Medium, Decem-

ber 17, 2018, https://medium.com/@egbunaoluebube/distracted-by-fame
-723477e9023b. Used and adapted by permission.

7. Egbuna, "Distracted by Fame?"

8. 1 Corinthians 13:13.

9. *The Works of Robert G. Ingersoll,* ed. C. P. Farrell, vol. 11 (New York: Dresden Publishing, 1902), www.gutenberg.org/files/38813/38813-h/38813
-h.htm#K.

## Chapter 9: Beaches Get Boring

1. Dorothy Sayers, "Why Work?" in *Letters to a Diminished Church: Passionate Arguments for the Relevance of Christian Doctrine* (1942; repr., Nashville: W Publishing Group, 2004), 118–25.

2. Gallup, *State of the Global Workplace* (New York: Gallup Press, 2017), 22–24. Data was aggregated from 2014 through 2016 across 155 countries. (1) "Engaged" employees are defined as "highly involved in and enthusiastic about their work and workplace. They are psychological 'owners,' drive performance and innovation, and move the organization forward." (2) "Not engaged" employees "are psychologically unattached to their work and company. Because their engagement needs are not being fully met, they're putting time—but not energy or passion—into their work." (3) "Actively disengaged" employees "aren't just unhappy at work—they are resentful that their needs aren't being met and are acting out their unhappiness. Every day, these workers potentially undermine what their engaged coworkers accomplish."

3. CareerBuilder, "Increased Number of Workers Calling in Sick When They Aren't, Finds CareerBuilder's Annual Survey," PR Newswire, November 16, 2017, www.prnewswire.com/news-releases/increased-number
-of-workers-calling-in-sick-when-they-arent-finds-careerbuilders-annual
-survey-300555582.html.

4. Zoya Gervis, "Here's How Many Days a Year the Average American Spends Daydreaming About a Vacation," SWNS Digital, October 24, 2019, www.swnsdigital.com/2019/10/heres-how-many-days-a-year-the
-average-american-spends-daydreaming-about-a-vacation.

5. Hannah Sampson, "What Does America Have Against Vacation?," *Washington Post,* August 28, 2019, www.washingtonpost.com/travel/2019/08
/28/what-does-america-have-against-vacation.

6. Sampson, "What Does America Have Against Vacation?"

7. Amanda Dixon, "Americans Reveal Ideal Ages for Financial Milestones,"

Bankrate, July 18, 2018, www.bankrate.com/personal-finance/smart
-money/financial-milestones-survey-july-2018.

8. Axel von Herbay, "Otto von Bismarck Is Not the Origin of Old Age at
65," *Gerontologist* 54, no. 1 (February 2014): 5, https://doi.org/10.1093
/geront/gnt111; and Social Security Administration, "Age 65 Retirement," www.ssa.gov/history/age65.html.

9. Aspen Gorry, Devon Gorry, and Sita Slavov, "Does Retirement Improve
Health and Life Satisfaction?," Working Paper 21326, National Bureau
of Economic Research, July 2015, doi:10.3386/w21326, www.nber.org
/papers/w21326.

10. Kathy Kristof, "Surprise—Money Doesn't Guarantee Happy Retirement.
Here's What Does," *Inc.*, March/April 2018, www.inc.com/magazine
/201804/kathy-kristof/happy-retirement-satisfaction-enjoy-life.html.

11. Stephen Wright, "The Difference Between Happy and Unhappy Retirees," *Pinnacle Quarterly,* Vision Wealth Planning, January 2020, 12,
https://static.twentyoverten.com/5a29586cd744f3738318b502/zeZKO7
CfW/VISION-Quarterly-Q1-2020.pdf (emphasis added).

12. Matt Clarke, "Long-Term Recidivism Studies Show High Arrest Rates,"
*Prison Legal News,* May 3, 2019, www.prisonlegalnews.org/news/2019
/may/3/long-term-recidivism-studies-show-high-arrest-rates.

## Chapter 10: Blinking Lights

1. Cal Newport, *Digital Minimalism: Choosing a Focused Life in a Noisy
World* (New York: Penguin, 2019), 8.

2. "The Nielsen Total Audience Report: August 2020," Nielsen, August 13,
2020, www.nielsen.com/us/en/insights/report/2020/the-nielsen-total
-audience-report-august-2020. The total time spent consuming media in
2020 had increased by nearly an hour a day over 2019, representing the
additional time Americans were spending with media during COVID-19
isolation. The survey also notes, "Some amount of simultaneous usage
may occur across devices."

3. Rani Molla, "Tech Companies Tried to Help Us Spend Less Time on Our
Phones. It Didn't Work," *Vox,* January 6, 2020, www.vox.com/recode
/2020/1/6/21048116/tech-companies-time-well-spent-mobile-phone
-usage-data. The figures on smartphone usage come from productivity
software company RescueTime.

4. J. R. Thorpe, "This Is What Too Much Screen Time Does to You," *Bustle,*
November 6, 2020, www.bustle.com/wellness/117838-5-things-too

-much-screen-time-does-to-your-body. See also Juliane Horvath et al., "Structural and Functional Correlates of Smartphone Addiction," *Addictive Behaviors* 105 (June 2020), https://doi.org/10.1016/j.addbeh.2020.106334.

5. Thorpe, "This Is What Too Much Screen Time Does to You." See also Xiao Wang, Yuexuan Li, and Haoliang Fan, "The Associations Between Screen Time–Based Sedentary Behavior and Depression: A Systematic Review and Meta-analysis," *BMC Public Health* 19, art. no. 1524 (2019), https://doi.org/10.1186/s12889-019-7904-9.

6. Moran Bodas et al., "Anxiety-Inducing Media: The Effect of Constant News Broadcasting on the Well-Being of Israeli Television Viewers," *Psychiatry* 78, no. 3 (2015): 265–76, https://doi.org/10.1080/00332747.2015.1069658.

7. Thorpe, "This Is What Too Much Screen Time Does to You." See also Eva M. Selhub and Alan C. Logan, *Your Brain on Nature: The Science of Nature's Influence on Your Health, Happiness, and Vitality* (Mississauga, Ontario, Canada: Wiley, 2012), 45.

8. Kermit Pattison, "Worker Interrupted: The Cost of Task Switching," *Fast Company,* July 28, 2018, www.fastcompany.com/944128/worker-interrupted-cost-task-switching. See also Gloria Mark, Daniela Gudith, and Ulrich Klocke, "The Cost of Interrupted Work: More Speed and Stress," *CHI '08: Proceedings of the SIGCHI Conference on Human Factors in Computing Systems* (April 6, 2008): 107–10, https://doi.org/10.1145/1357054.1357072.

9. Nicholas Carr, *The Shallows: What the Internet Is Doing to Our Brains,* updated ed. (New York: Norton, 2020), 10.

10. Cal Newport, *Deep Work: Rules for Focused Success in a Distracted World* (New York: Grand Central, 2016).

11. Cal Newport, quoted in Eric Barker, "Stay Focused: 5 Ways to Increase Your Attention Span," *Time,* June 26, 2014, https://time.com/2921341/stay-focused-5-ways-to-increase-your-attention-span.

12. Newport, *Digital Minimalism,* 6–7.

13. Newport, *Digital Minimalism,* 9.

14. Lydia Belanger, "10 Ways Technology Hijacks Your Behavior," *Entrepreneur,* April 3, 2018, www.entrepreneur.com/article/311284.

15. Avery Hartmans, "These Are the Sneaky Ways Apps Like Instagram, Facebook, Tinder Lure You in and Get You 'Addicted,'" Insider, February 17, 2018, www.businessinsider.com/how-app-developers-keep-us-addicted-to-our-smartphones-2018-1.

16. Adam Alter, *Irresistible: The Rise of Addictive Technology and the Business of Keeping Us Hooked* (New York: Penguin, 2018), 10.

17. Nir Eyal, *Indistractable: How to Control Your Attention and Choose Your Life* (London: Bloomsbury, 2019), 2.

18. Tristan Harris, quoted in Alex Kantrowitz, " 'Social Dilemma' Star Tristan Harris Responds to Criticisms of the Film, Netflix's Algorithm, and More," *OneZero*, October 7, 2020, https://onezero.medium.com /social-dilemma-star-tristan-harris-responds-to-criticisms-of-the-film-netflix -s-algorithm-and-e11c3bedd3eb.

## Chapter 11: Live the Story You Want Told

1. "UNICEF and global partners define an orphan as a child under eighteen years of age who has lost one or both parents to any cause of death. By this definition, there were nearly 140 million orphans globally in 2015, including 61 million in Asia, 52 million in Africa, 10 million in Latin America and the Caribbean, and 7.3 million in Eastern Europe and Central Asia." "Orphans," UNICEF, https://web.archive.org/web/20210614053425/www .unicef.org/media/orphans.

## Bonus Exercise: Discover Your Purposes

1. Dictionary.com, s.v. "work," www.dictionary.com/browse/work.

Joshua Becker is the bestselling author of *The Minimalist Home, The More of Less,* and *Simplify.*

He is the founder and editor of *Becoming Minimalist,* a website dedicated to intentional living visited by over 1.5 million readers every month with a social media following of over 3 million. His blog was named by *SUCCESS* magazine as one of the top ten personal-development websites on the internet, and his writing has been featured in publications all around the world.

He is the creator of *Simplify* magazine and *Simple Money* magazine and a contributing writer for *Forbes.*

Joshua and his young family were introduced to minimalism during a short conversation with their neighbor. Since then, Joshua's story and writing have inspired millions around the world to find more life by owning fewer possessions. Today, based on his thoughtful and intentional approach to minimalism, he is one of the leading voices in the modern simplicity movement.

He is also the founder of the Hope Effect, a nonprofit organization changing how the world cares for orphans.

His online course, Uncluttered, has helped over seventy thousand people declutter their homes and live more intentional lives focused on the things that matter most. His app, Clutterfree, is the only app to create a personalized room-by-room decluttering to-do list for an individual's home.

Joshua lives in Peoria, Arizona, with his wife and two teenage kids.

Visit his website: www.becomingminimalist.com.

# LIVE THE INTENTIONAL LIFE

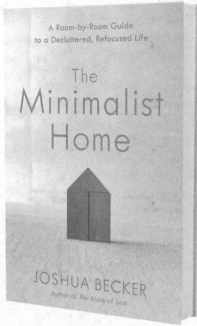

Be known for the life you live, not the things you own. Uncover your life, pursue your passion, and overcome a world focused on all the wrong things. Rethink the common assumptions of today and find satisfaction and fulfillment tomorrow.

becoming
**(( ● minimalist**.com

Becoming Minimalist *inspires others to live more by owning less. The website is home to over 1 million readers per month who recognize life is too valuable to waste chasing material possessions.*

*With encouragement, inspiration, and practical advice, it encourages each reader to discover the life-giving benefits of owning less by removing the distraction of physical possessions.*

— —

## OTHER RESOURCES:

**YouTube:** Hundreds of free videos to help you remove distractions and live a more intentional life. Learn more at youtube.com/c/JoshuaBecker.

**The Uncluttered Course:** A 12-week, self-guided, online course designed to help you own less, live more, and discover the life you've always wanted. Discover more at my.becomingminimalist.com.

*Simplify Magazine:* A quarterly digital publication that pulls together experts in various fields to address some of the most pressing needs of the modern family. Find out more at simplifymagazine.com.

**The Clutterfree App:** The first and only handheld app to create a personalized, step-by-step road map to declutter your unique home. Track your progress, find inspiration, complete challenges, and discover specific bonus plans for your home's toughest decluttering spaces. Available for download on the App Store and Google Play Store.

— —

**THE HOPE EFFECT:** As mentioned in *Things That Matter*, this nonprofit organization founded by Joshua and Kim is changing the way the world cares for orphans, because every child deserves a family. You can join the cause at hopeeffect.com.